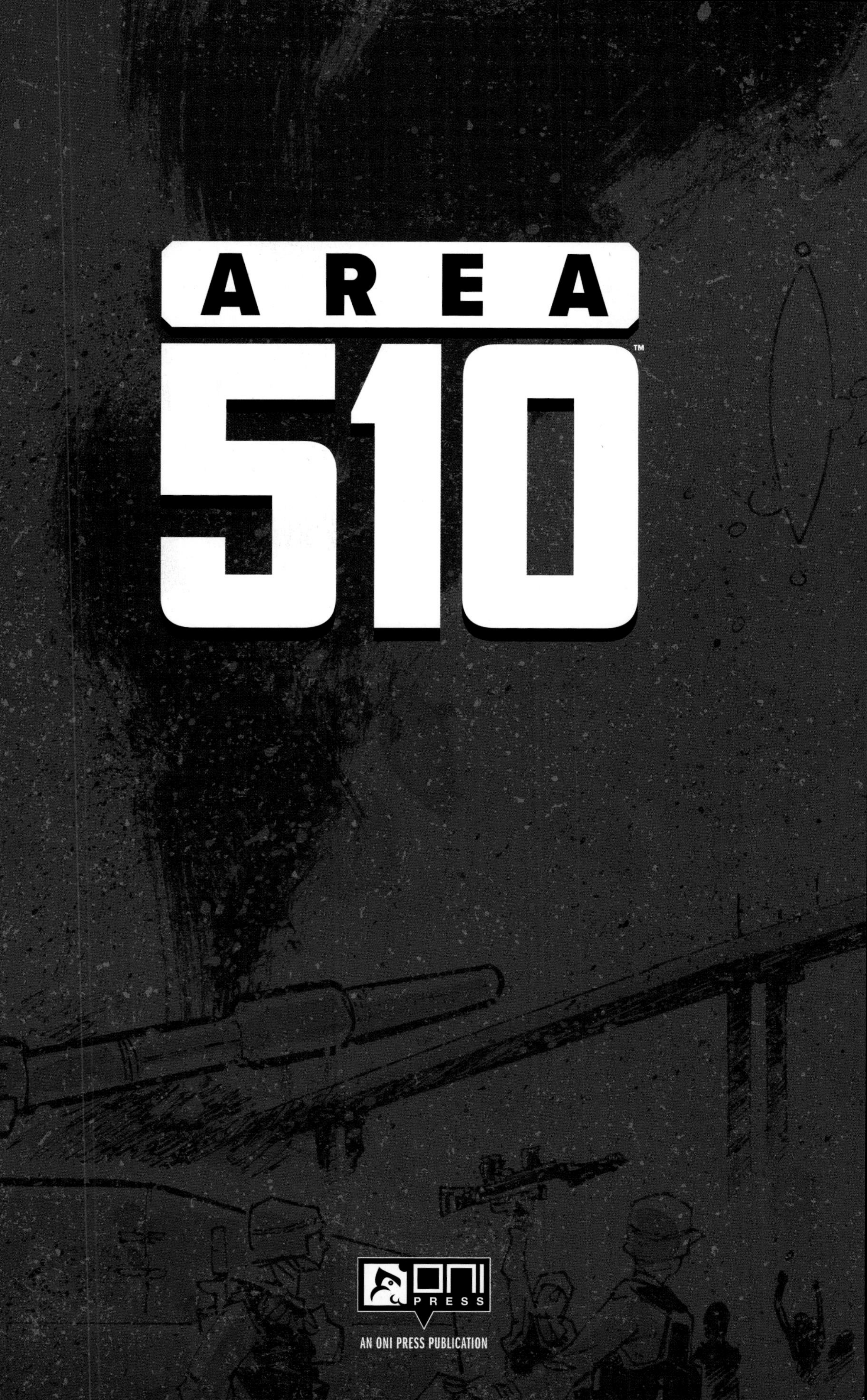
AREA
510™
ONI PRESS
AN ONI PRESS PUBLICATION

AREA 510

written by
JAY FAERBER

illustrated by
JUSTIN GREENWOOD

colors by
LEE LOUGHRIDGE

letters by
THOMAS MAUER

Designed by
KEITH WOOD

Edited by
ROBERT MEYERS, CHRIS CERASI,
and GABRIEL GRANILLO

AN ONI PRESS PUBLICATION

Published by Oni-Lion Forge Publishing Group, LLC.

JAMES LUCAS JONES, *president & publisher*

CHARLIE CHU, *e.v.p. of creative & business development*

STEVE ELLIS, *s.v.p. of games & operations*

ALEX SEGURA, *s.v.p. of marketing & sales*

MICHELLE NGUYEN, *associate publisher*

BRAD ROOKS, *director of operations*

AMBER O'NEILL, *special projects manager*

KATIE SAINZ, *director of marketing*

TARA LEHMANN, *publicity director*

HENRY BARAJAS, *sales manager*

HOLLY AITCHISON, *consumer marketing manager*

LYDIA NGUYEN, *marketing intern*

TROY LOOK, *director of design & production*

ANGIE KNOWLES, *production manager*

KATE Z. STONE, *senior graphic designer*

CAREY HALL, *graphic designer*

SARAH ROCKWELL, *graphic designer*

HILARY THOMPSON, *graphic designer*

VINCENT KUKUA, *digital prepress technician*

CHRIS CERASI, *managing editor*

JASMINE AMIRI, *senior editor*

AMANDA MEADOWS, *senior editor*

BESS PALLARES, *editor*

DESIREE RODRIGUEZ, *editor*

GRACE SCHEIPETER, *editor*

ZACK SOTO, *editor*

GABRIEL GRANILLO, *editorial assistant*

BEN EISNER, *game developer*

SARA HARDING, *entertainment executive assistant*

JUNG LEE, *logistics coordinator*

KUIAN KELLUM, *warehouse assistant*

JOE NOZEMACK, *publisher emeritus*

1319 SE Martin Luther King Jr. Blvd.
Suite 240
Portland, OR 97214

onipress.com
facebook.com/onipress
twitter.com/onipress
instagram.com/onipress

First Edition: October 2022

ISBN 978-1-63715-087-0
eISBN 978-1-63715-107-5

10 9 8 7 6 5 4 3 2 1

Library of Congress Control Number: 2022932152

Printed in China

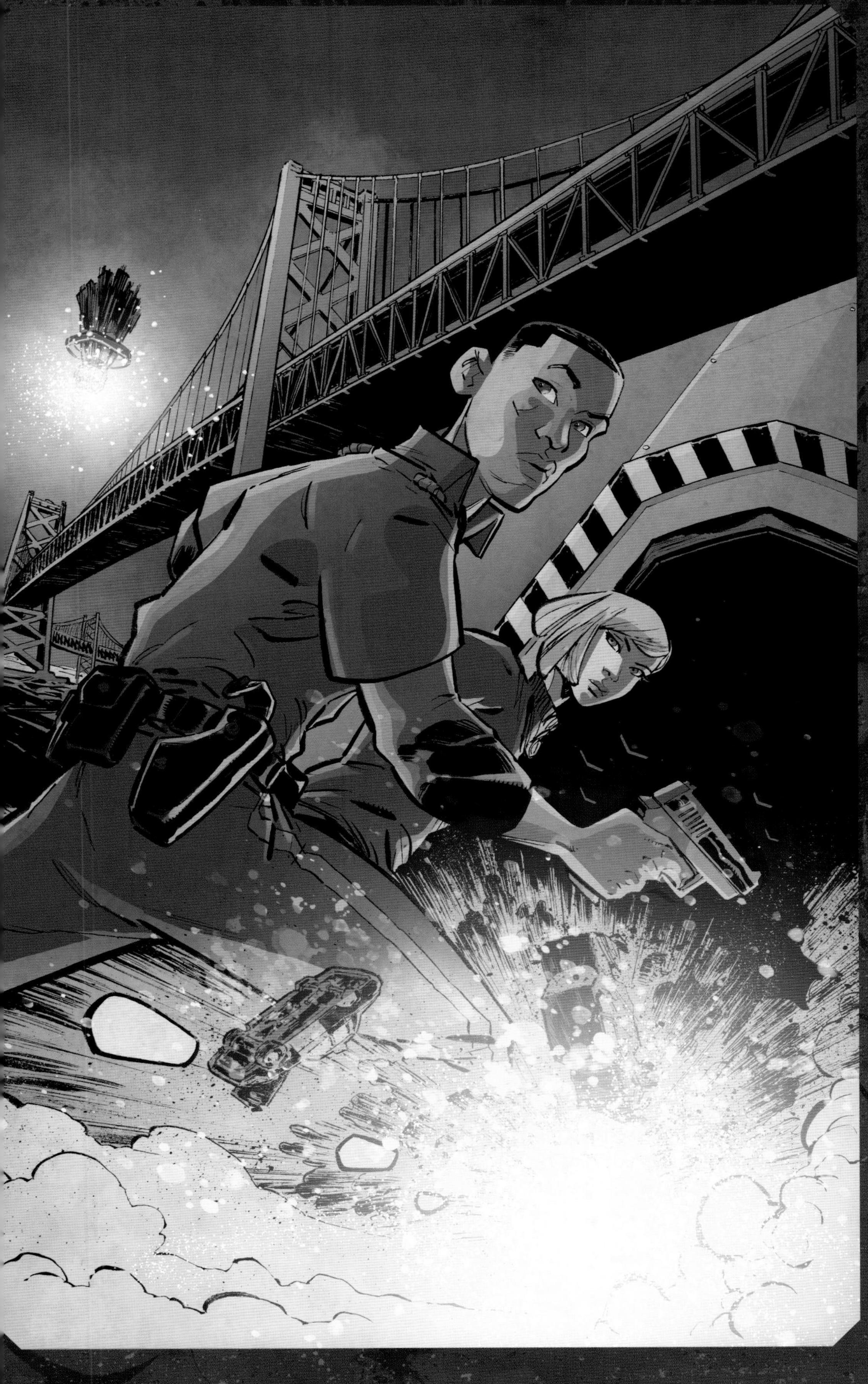

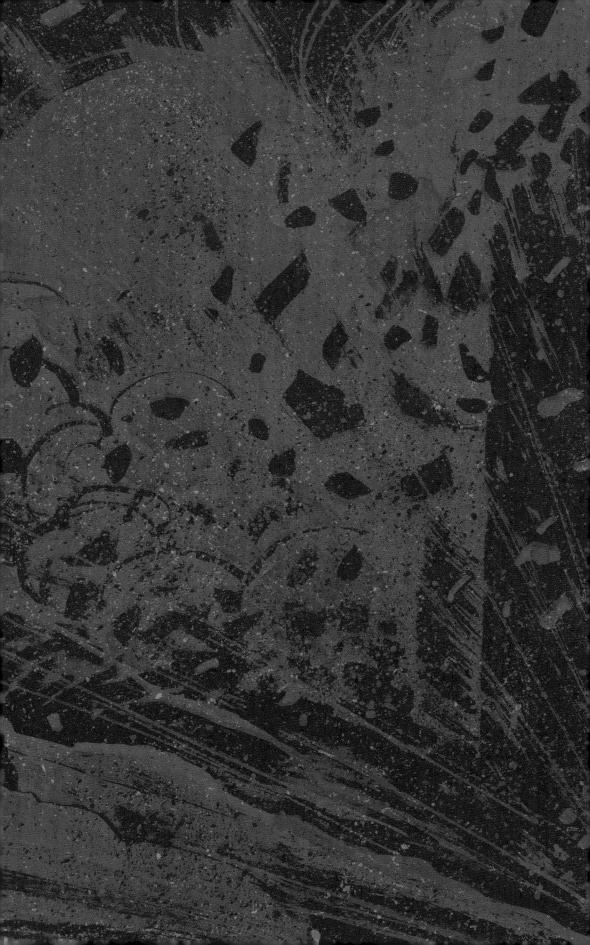

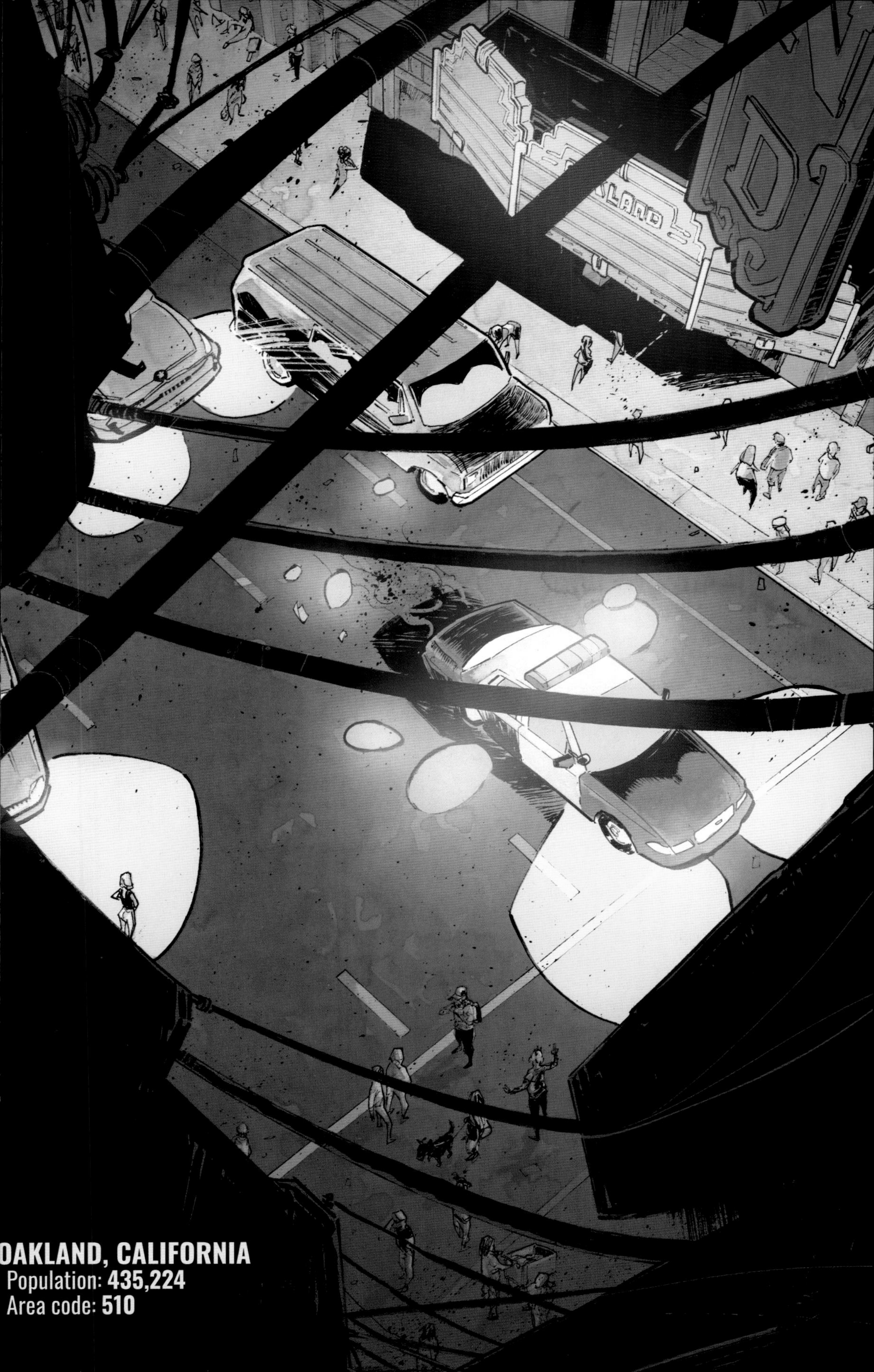
OAKLAND, CALIFORNIA
Population: 435,224
Area code: 510

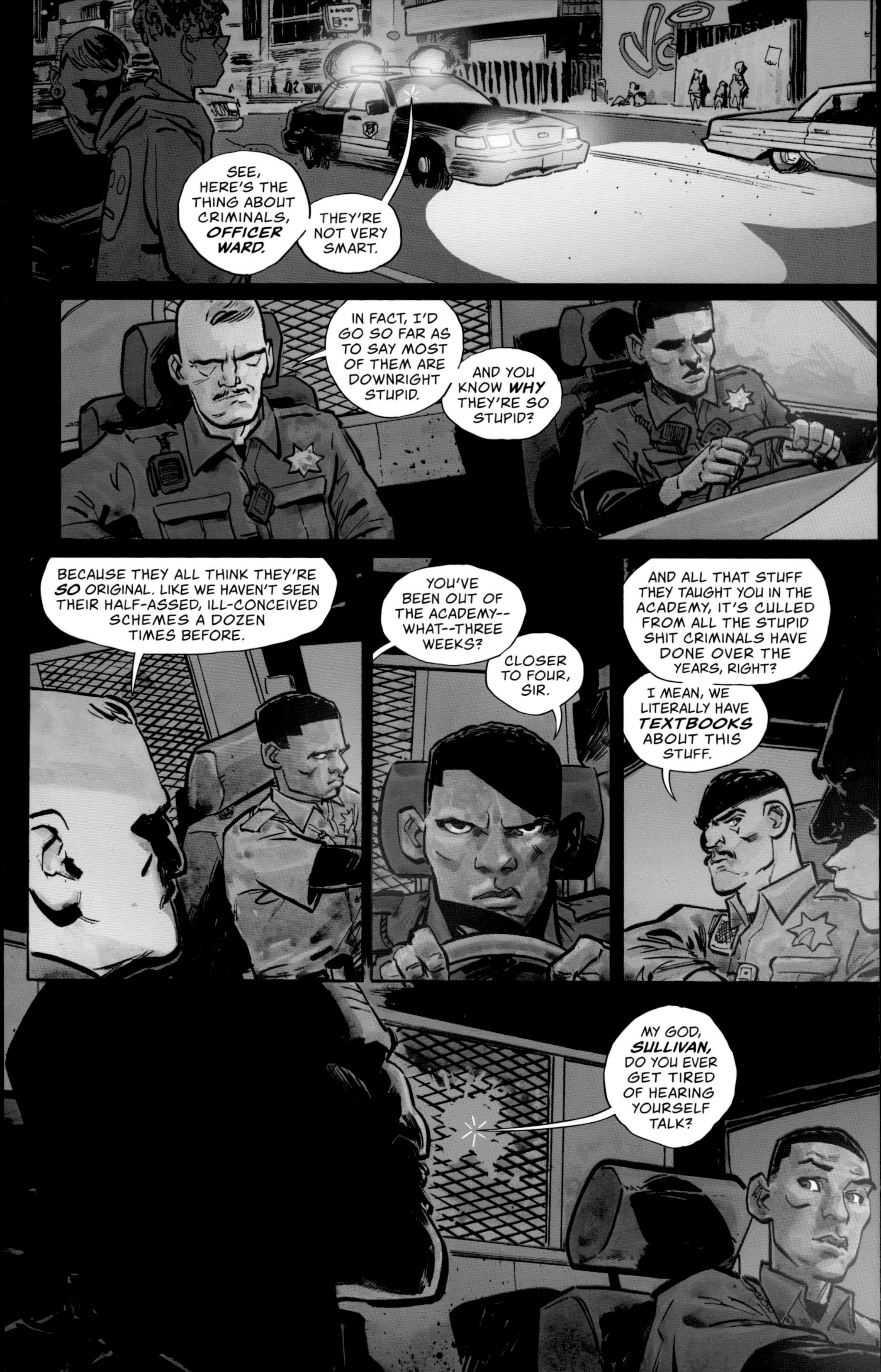
SEE, HERE'S THE THING ABOUT CRIMINALS, OFFICER WARD.
THEY'RE NOT VERY SMART.
IN FACT, I'D GO SO FAR AS TO SAY MOST OF THEM ARE DOWNRIGHT STUPID.
AND YOU KNOW WHY THEY'RE SO STUPID?
BECAUSE THEY ALL THINK THEY'RE SO ORIGINAL. LIKE WE HAVEN'T SEEN THEIR HALF-ASSED, ILL-CONCEIVED SCHEMES A DOZEN TIMES BEFORE.
YOU'VE BEEN OUT OF THE ACADEMY-- WHAT--THREE WEEKS?
CLOSER TO FOUR, SIR.
AND ALL THAT STUFF THEY TAUGHT YOU IN THE ACADEMY, IT'S CULLED FROM ALL THE STUPID SHIT CRIMINALS HAVE DONE OVER THE YEARS, RIGHT?
I MEAN, WE LITERALLY HAVE TEXTBOOKS ABOUT THIS STUFF.
MY GOD, SULLIVAN, DO YOU EVER GET TIRED OF HEARING YOURSELF TALK?

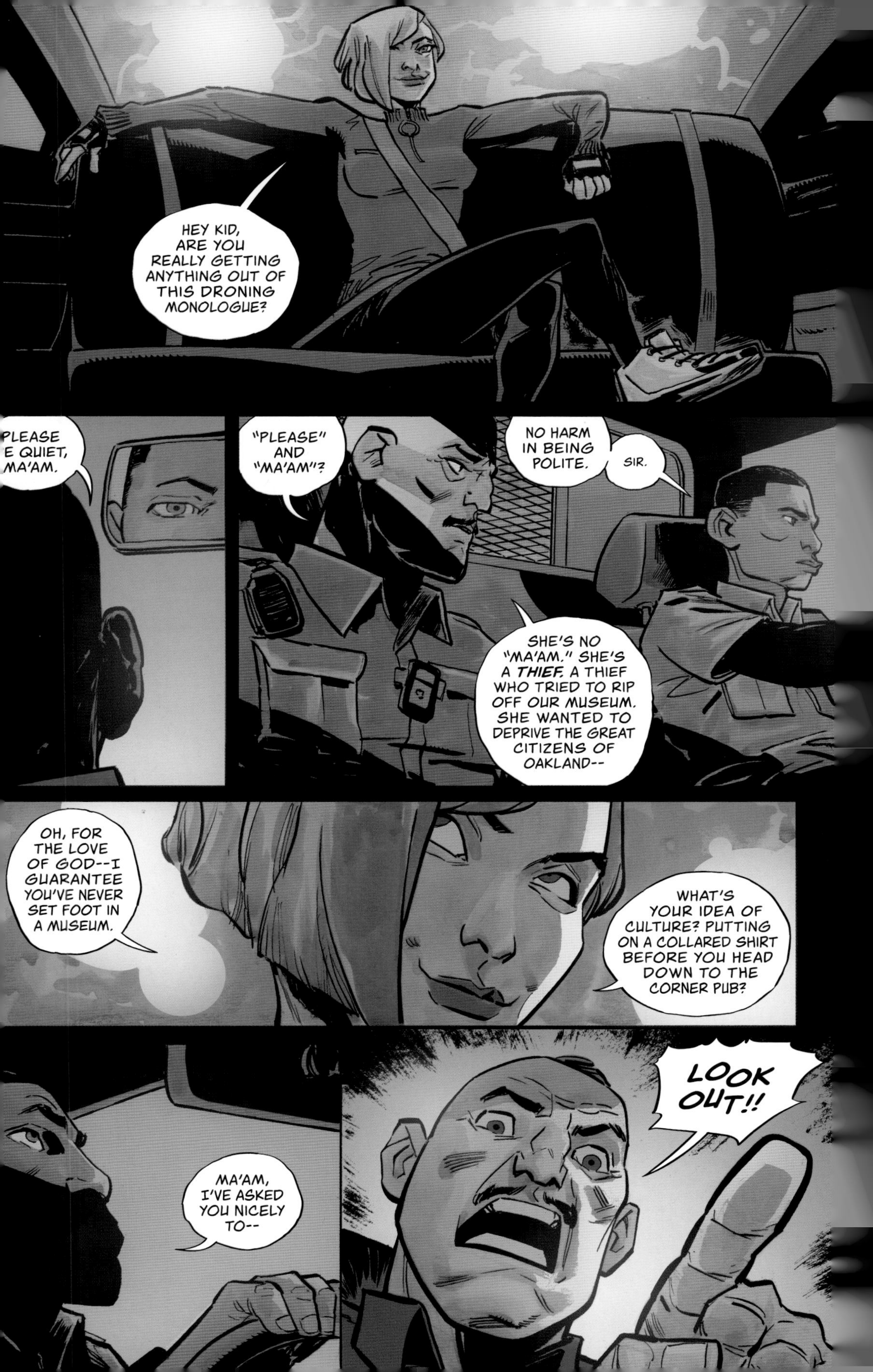
HEY KID, ARE YOU REALLY GETTING ANYTHING OUT OF THIS DRONING MONOLOGUE?
PLEASE E QUIET, MA'AM.
"PLEASE" AND "MA'AM"?
NO HARM IN BEING POLITE.
SIR.
SHE'S NO "MA'AM." SHE'S A *THIEF.* A THIEF WHO TRIED TO RIP OFF OUR MUSEUM. SHE WANTED TO DEPRIVE THE GREAT CITIZENS OF OAKLAND--
OH, FOR THE LOVE OF GOD--I GUARANTEE YOU'VE NEVER SET FOOT IN A MUSEUM.
WHAT'S YOUR IDEA OF CULTURE? PUTTING ON A COLLARED SHIRT BEFORE YOU HEAD DOWN TO THE CORNER PUB?
MA'AM, I'VE ASKED YOU NICELY TO--
LOOK OUT!!

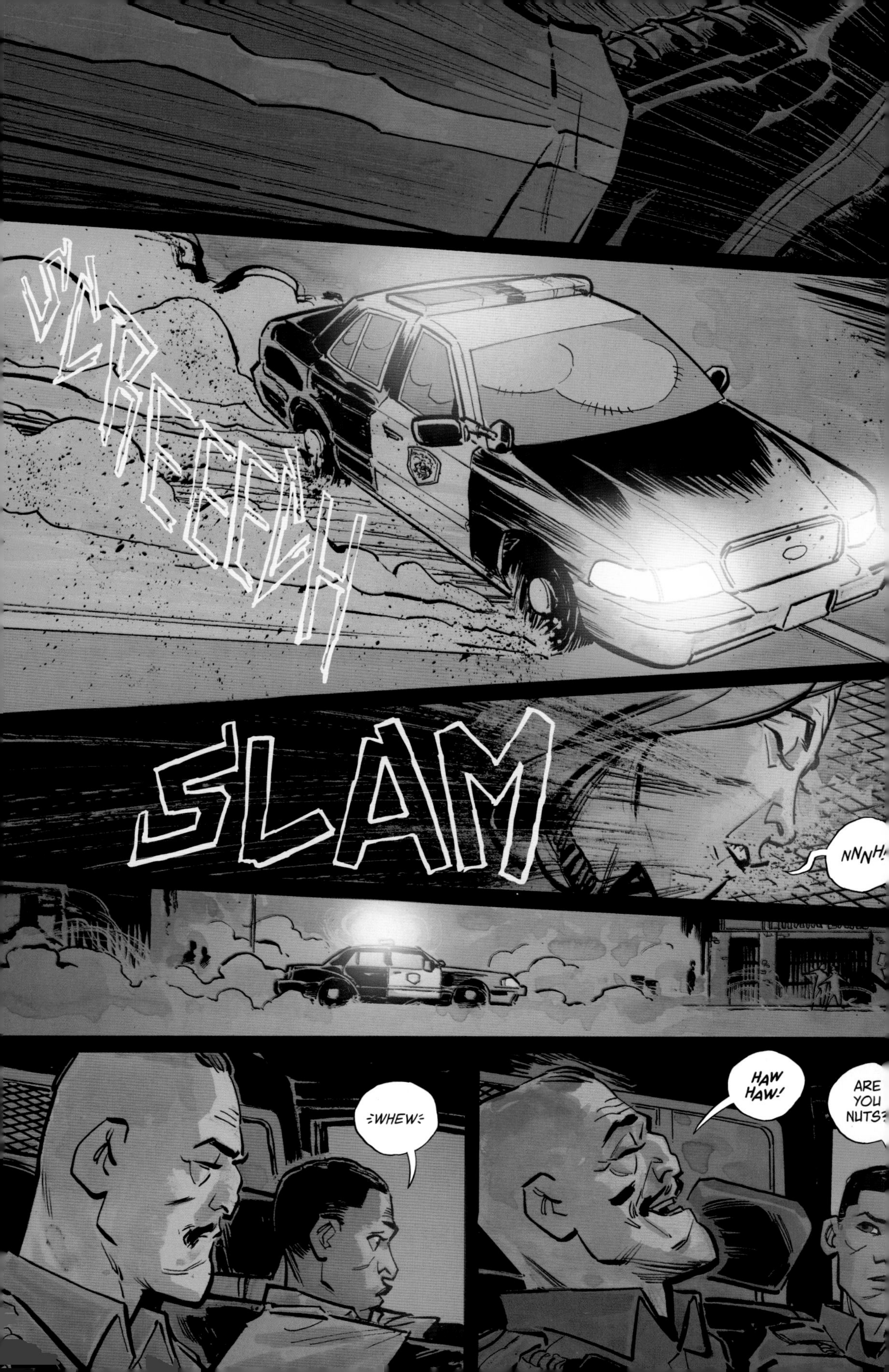
SCREEECH
SLAM
NNNH!
WHEW
HAW HAW!
ARE YOU NUTS?

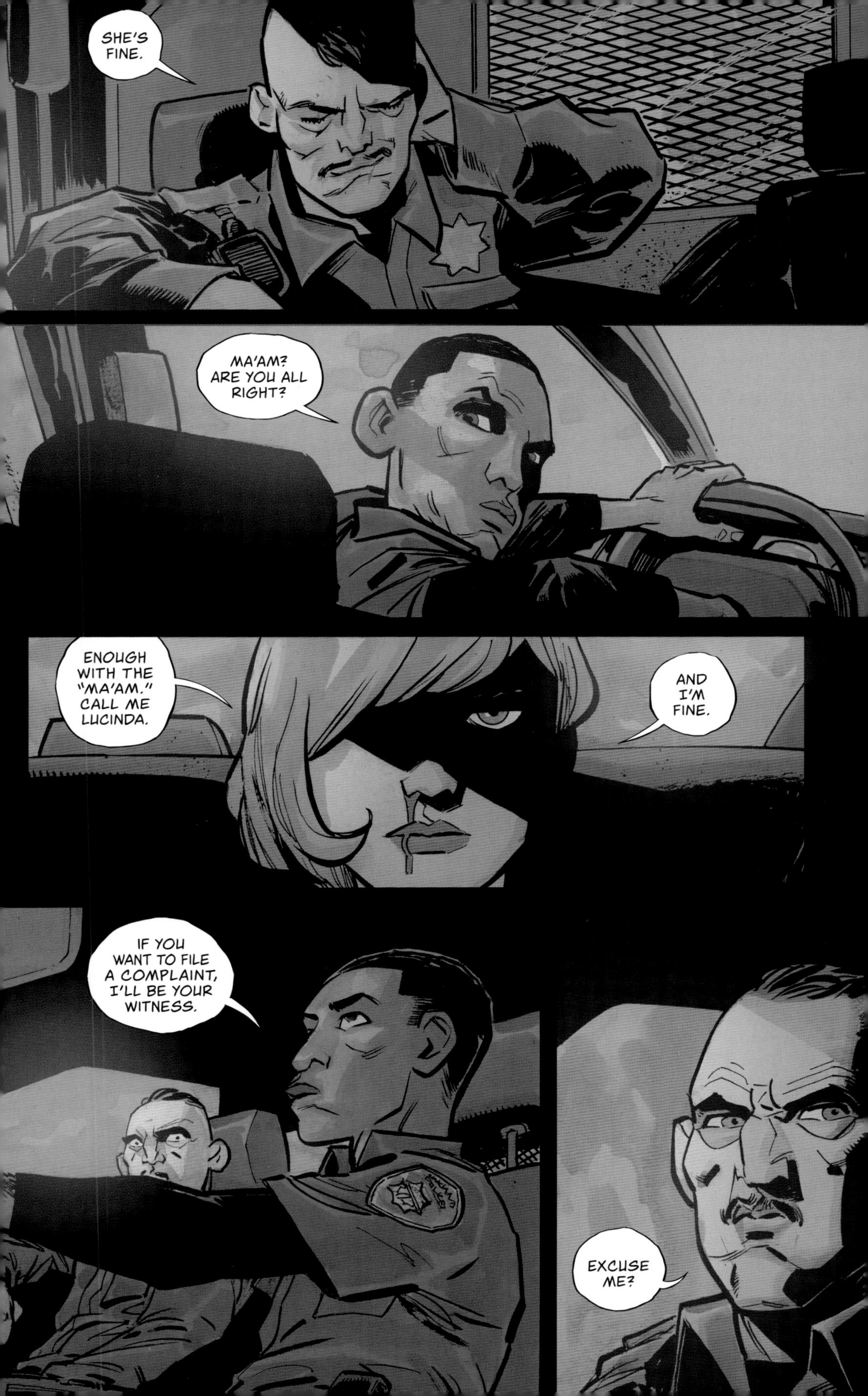
SHE'S FINE.
MA'AM? ARE YOU ALL RIGHT?
ENOUGH WITH THE "MA'AM." CALL ME LUCINDA.
AND I'M FINE.
IF YOU WANT TO FILE A COMPLAINT, I'LL BE YOUR WITNESS.
EXCUSE ME?

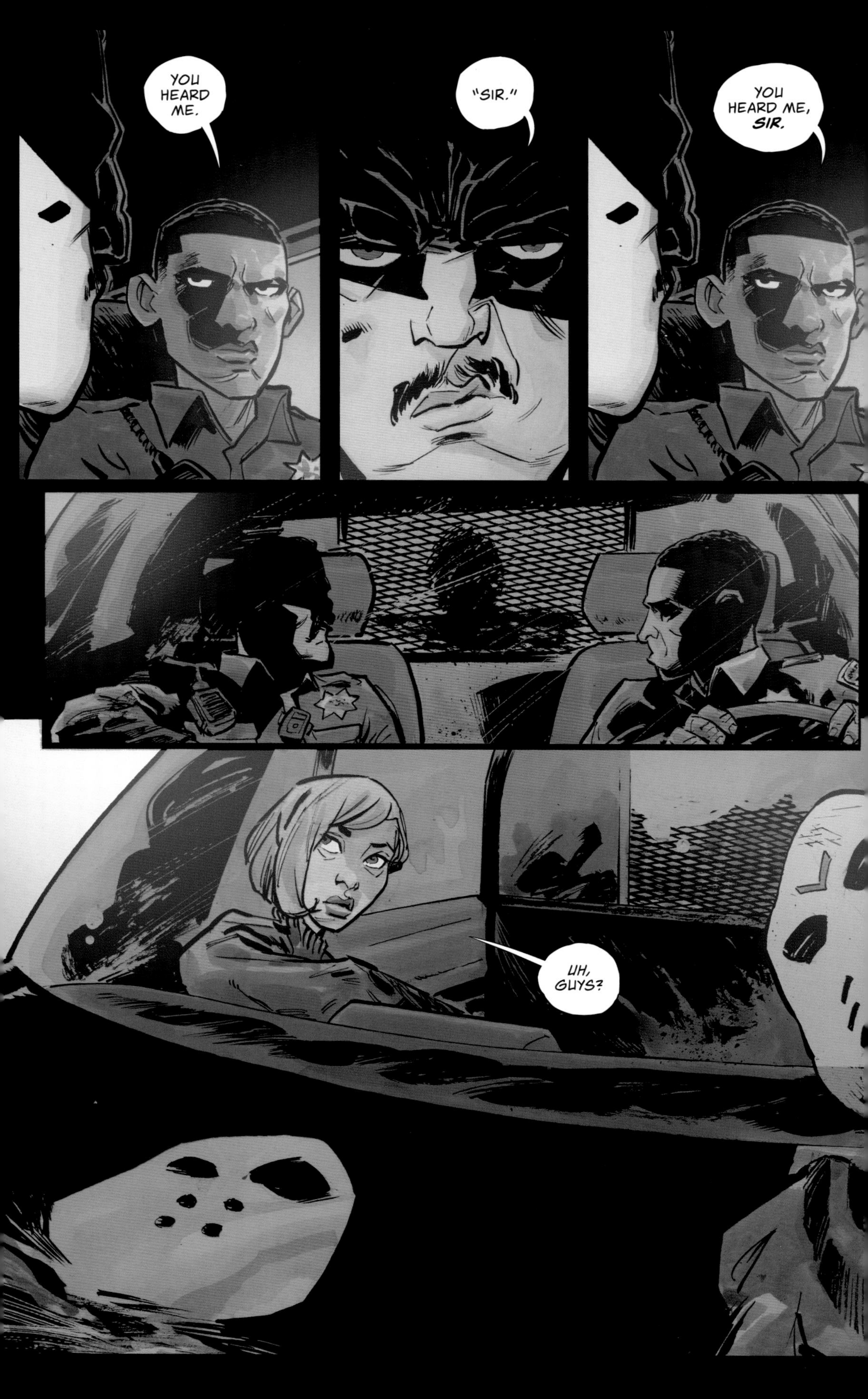
YOU HEARD ME.
"SIR."
YOU HEARD ME, SIR.
UH, GUYS?

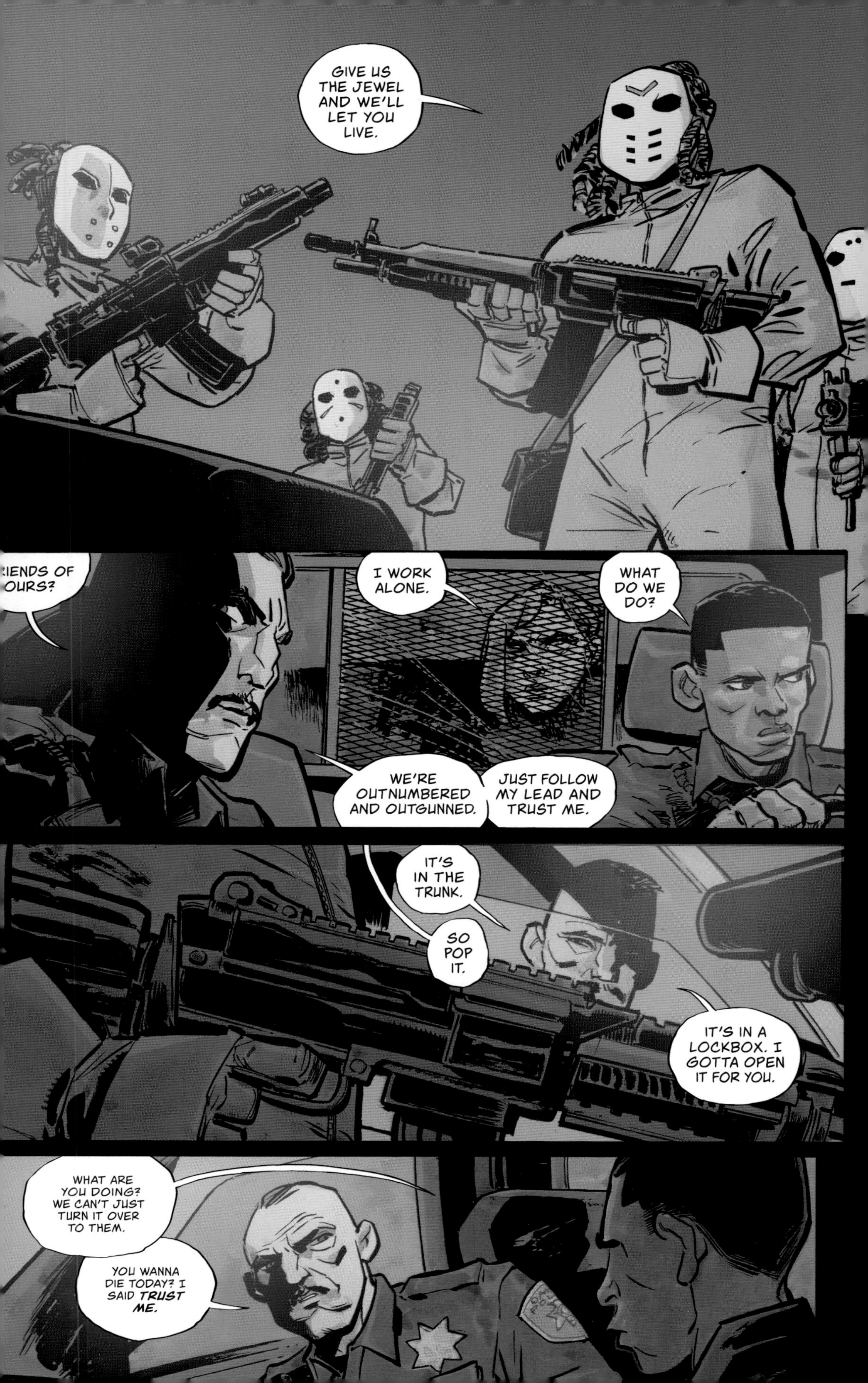
GIVE US THE JEWEL AND WE'LL LET YOU LIVE.
RIENDS OF OURS?
I WORK ALONE.
WHAT DO WE DO?
WE'RE OUTNUMBERED AND OUTGUNNED.
JUST FOLLOW MY LEAD AND TRUST ME.
IT'S IN THE TRUNK.
SO POP IT.
IT'S IN A LOCKBOX. I GOTTA OPEN IT FOR YOU.
WHAT ARE YOU DOING? WE CAN'T JUST TURN IT OVER TO THEM.
YOU WANNA DIE TODAY? I SAID *TRUST ME.*

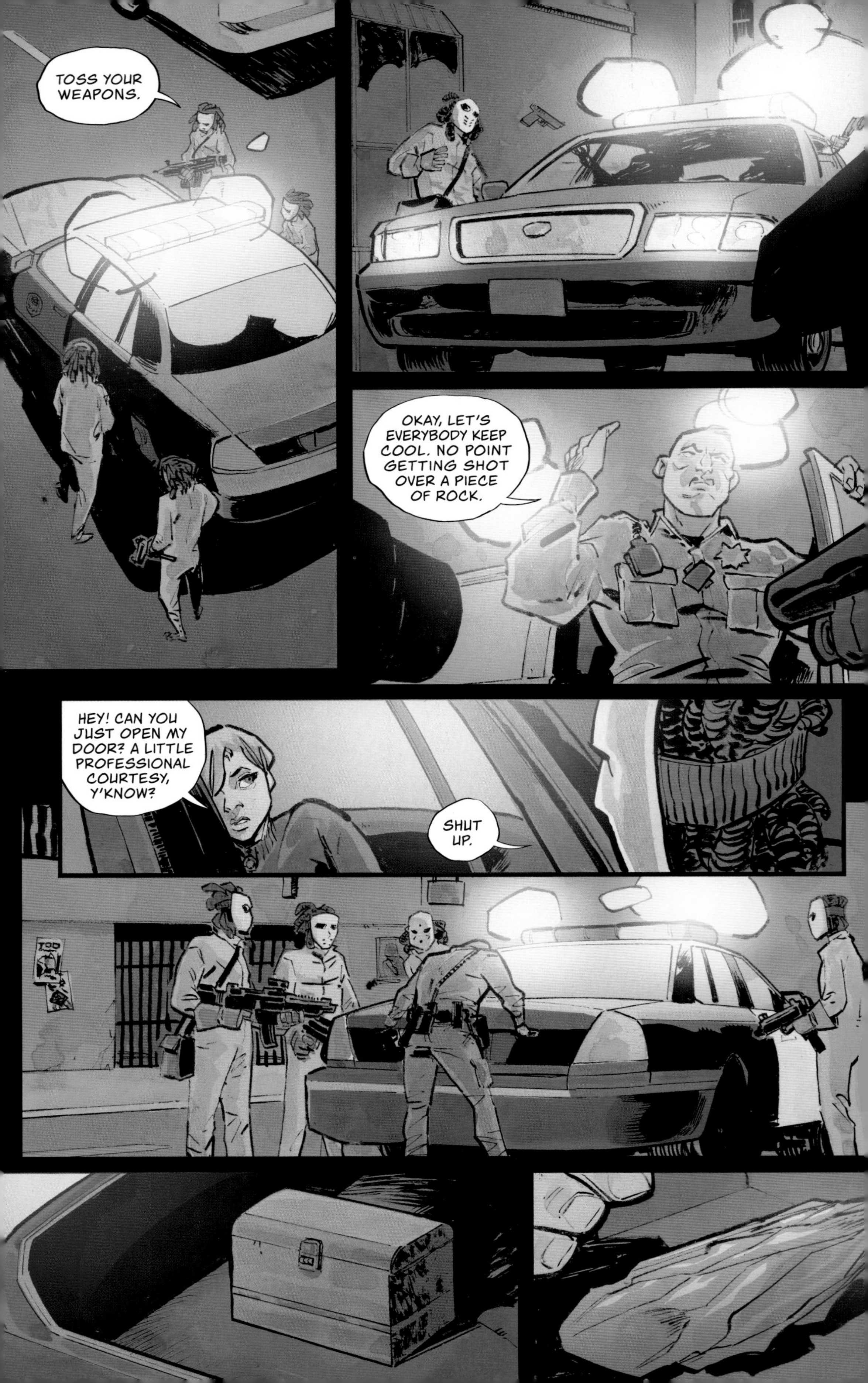
TOSS YOUR WEAPONS.
OKAY, LET'S EVERYBODY KEEP COOL. NO POINT GETTING SHOT OVER A PIECE OF ROCK.
HEY! CAN YOU JUST OPEN MY DOOR? A LITTLE PROFESSIONAL COURTESY, Y'KNOW?
SHUT UP.

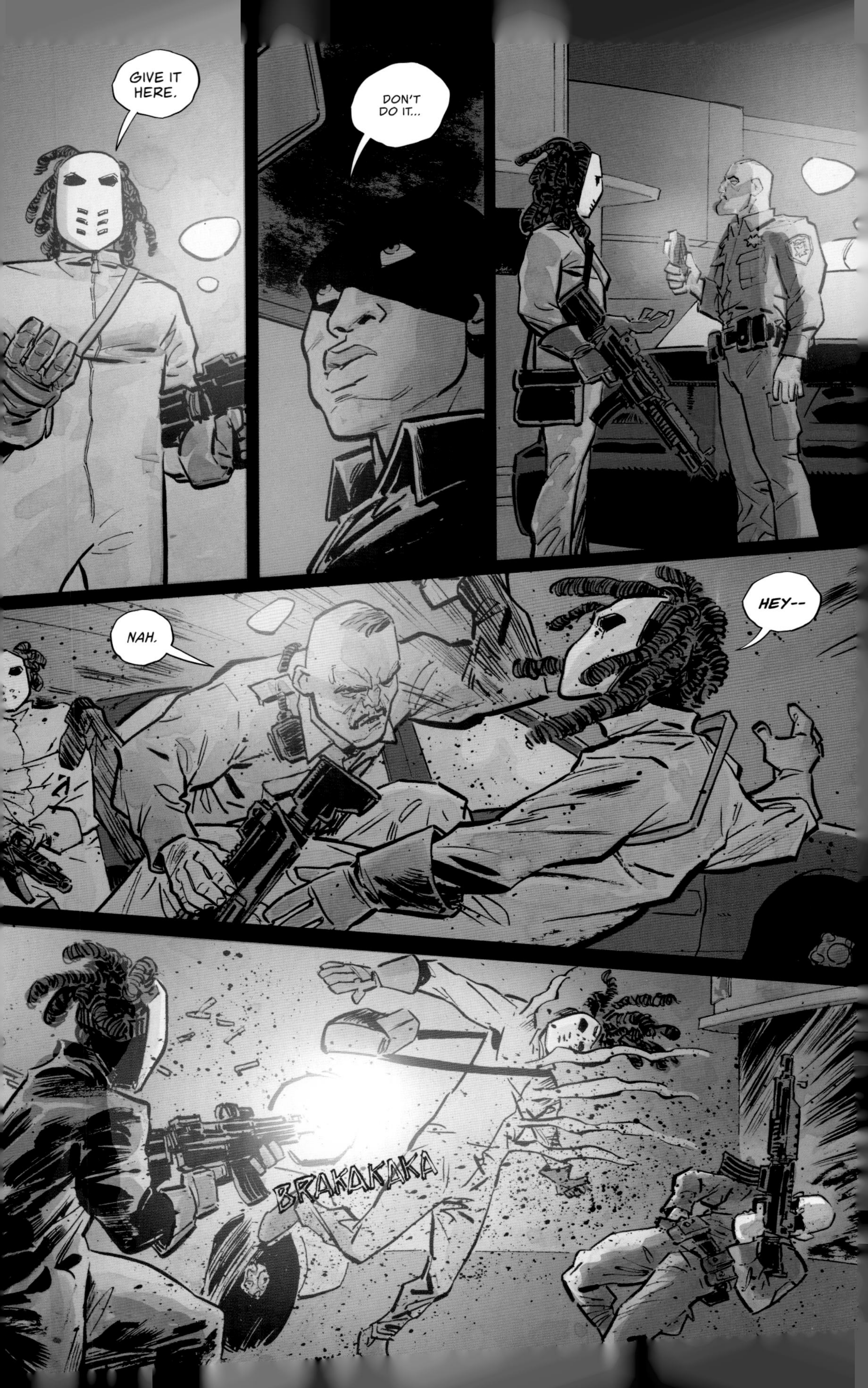
GIVE IT HERE.
DON'T DO IT...
NAH.
HEY--
BRAKAKAKA

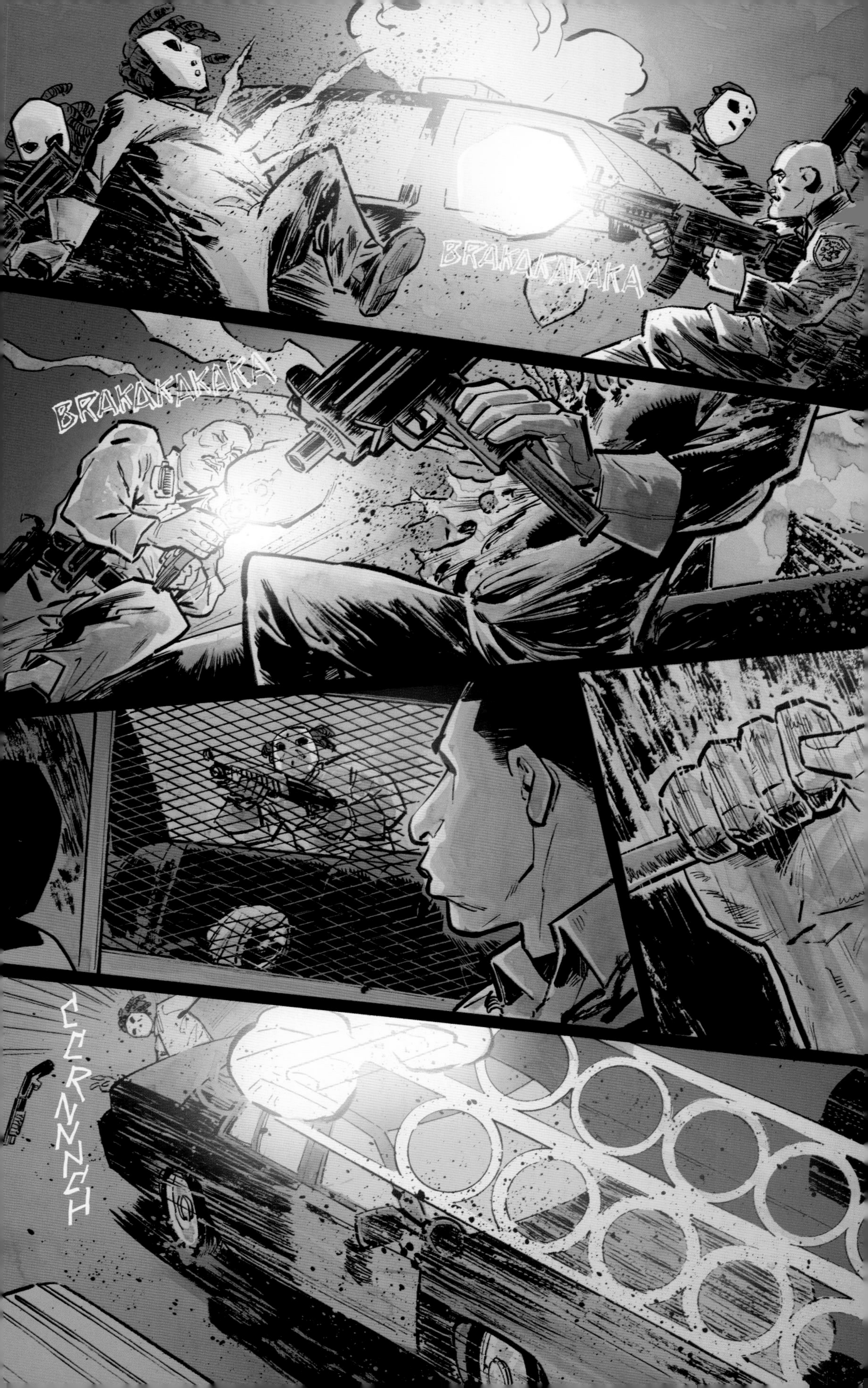
BRAKAKAKAKA
BRAKAKAKAKA
CCRNNNCH

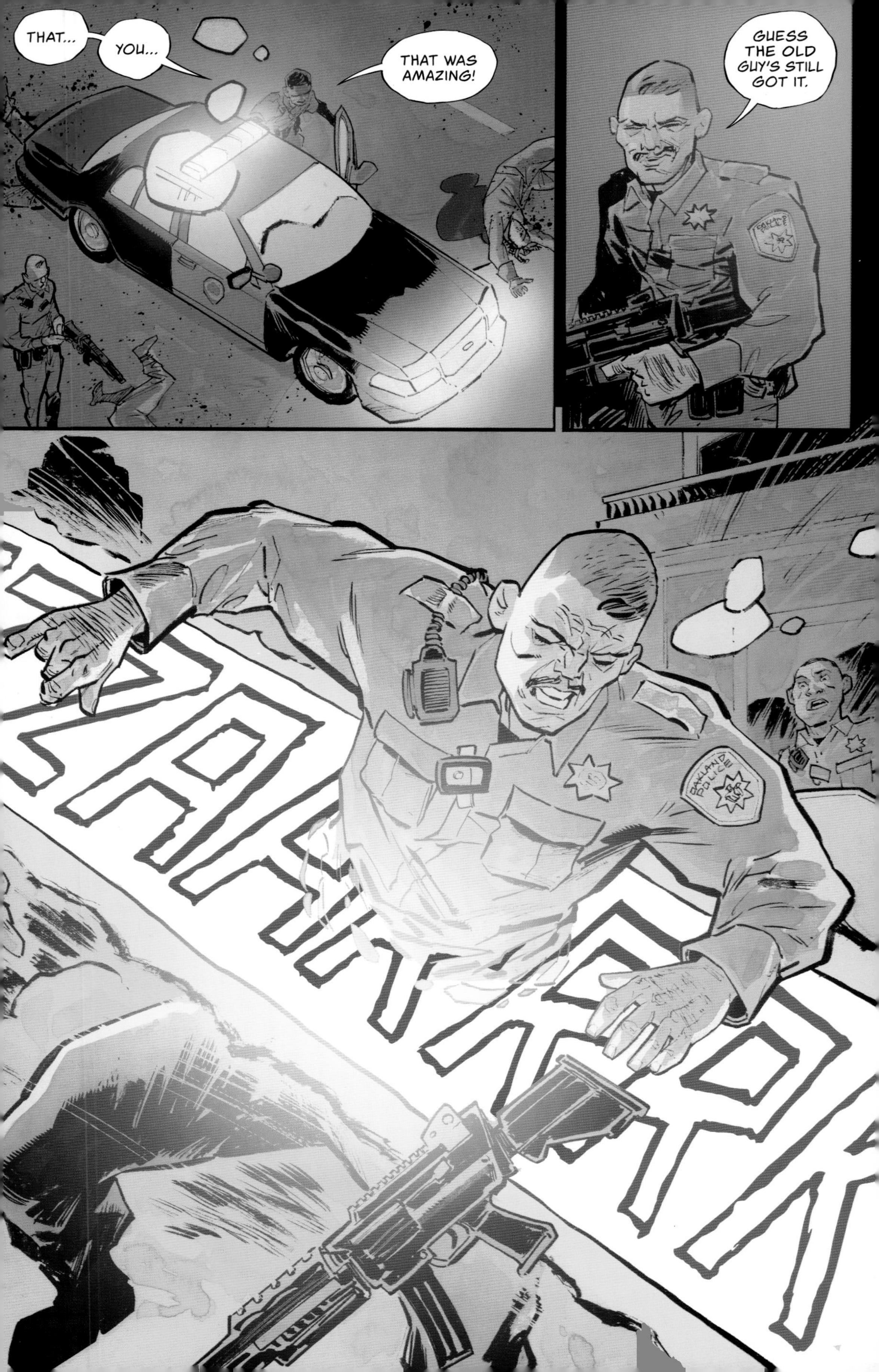
THAT...
YOU...
THAT WAS AMAZING!
GUESS THE OLD GUY'S STILL GOT IT.

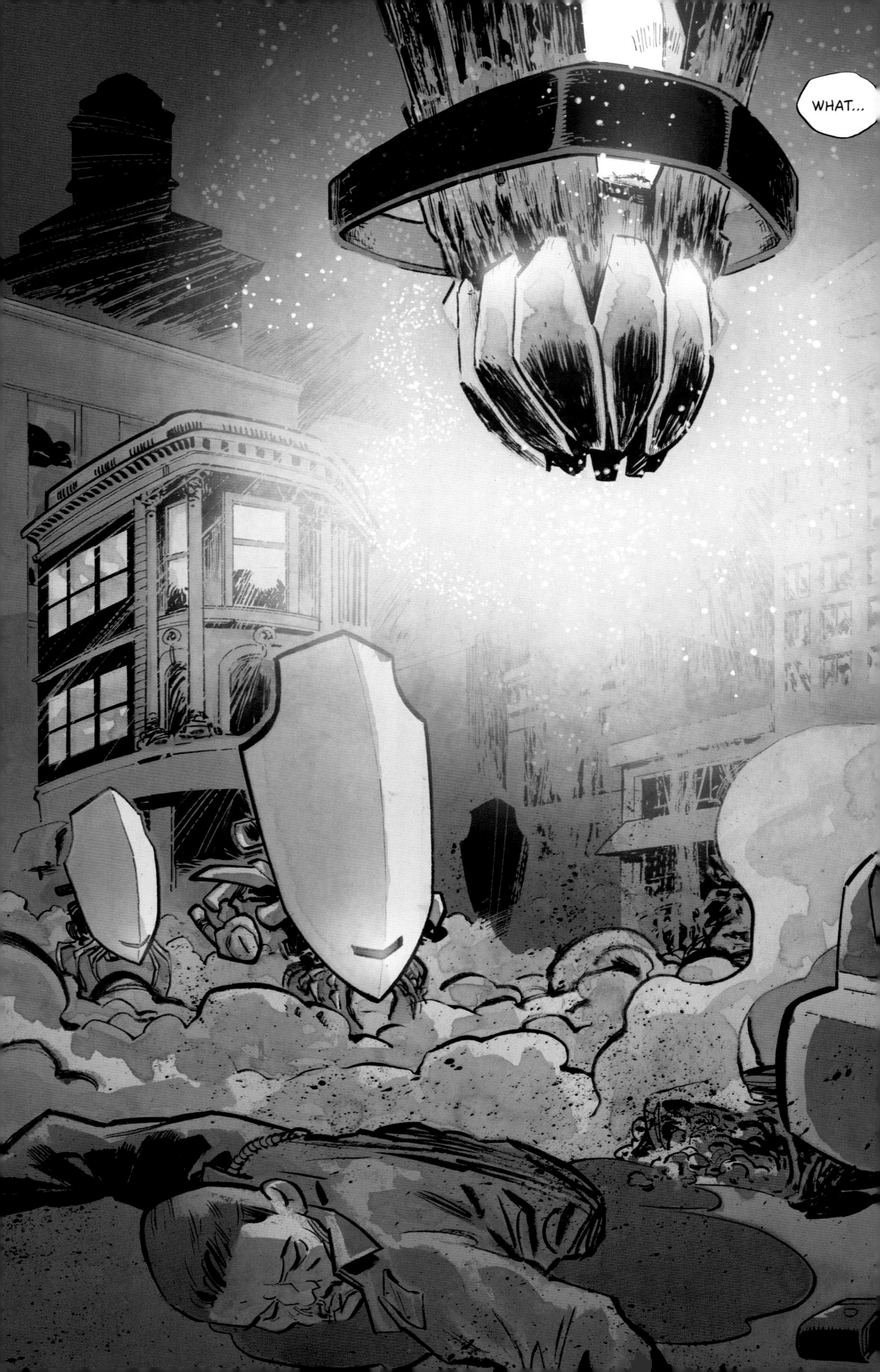
WHAT...

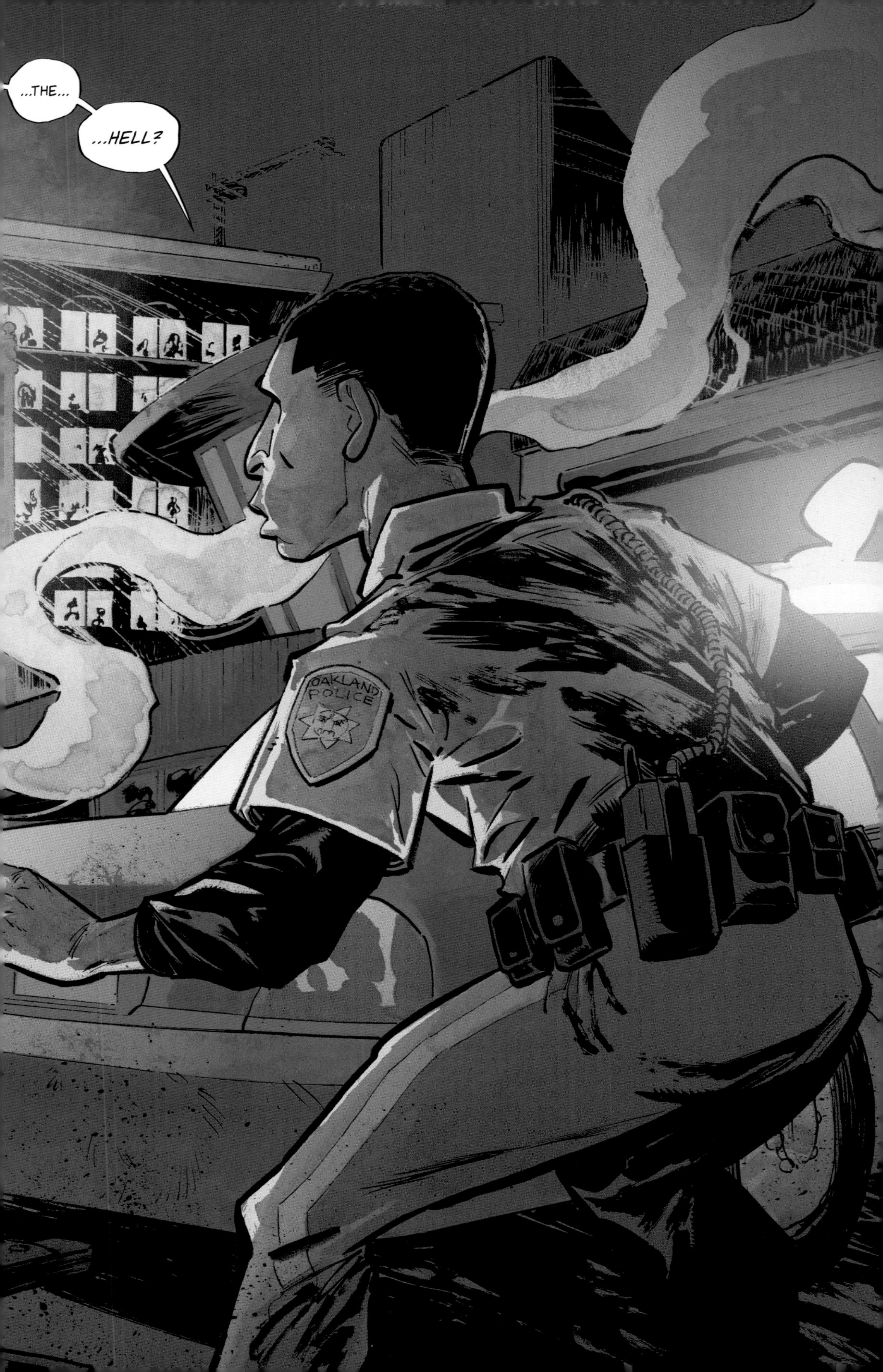
...THE...
...HELL?
OAKLAND POLICE

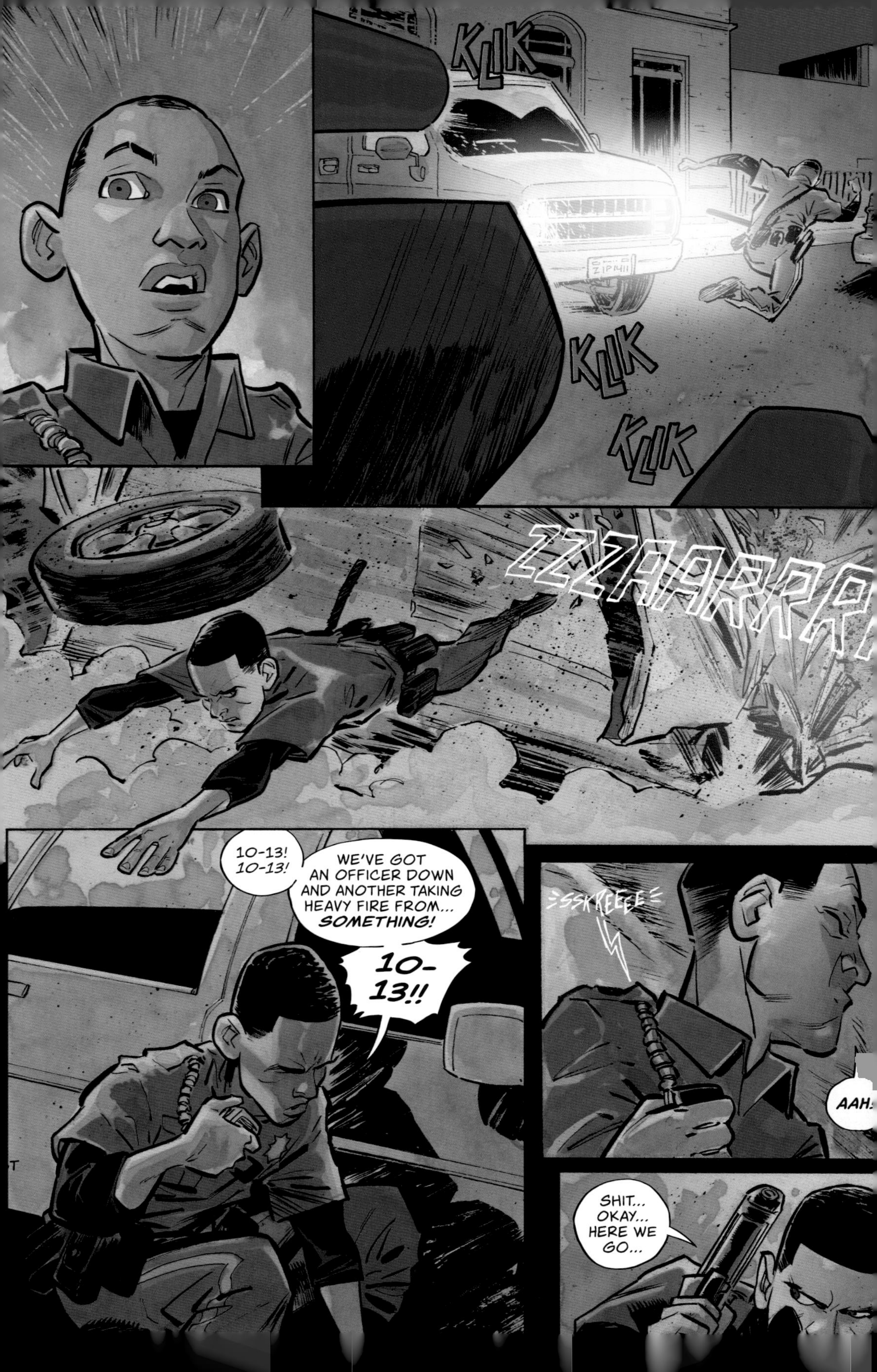
KLIK
KLIK
KLIK
ZZZAARRR
10-13! 10-13!
WE'VE GOT AN OFFICER DOWN AND ANOTHER TAKING HEAVY FIRE FROM... SOMETHING!
10-13!!
SSKREEEE
AAH
SHIT... OKAY... HERE WE GO...

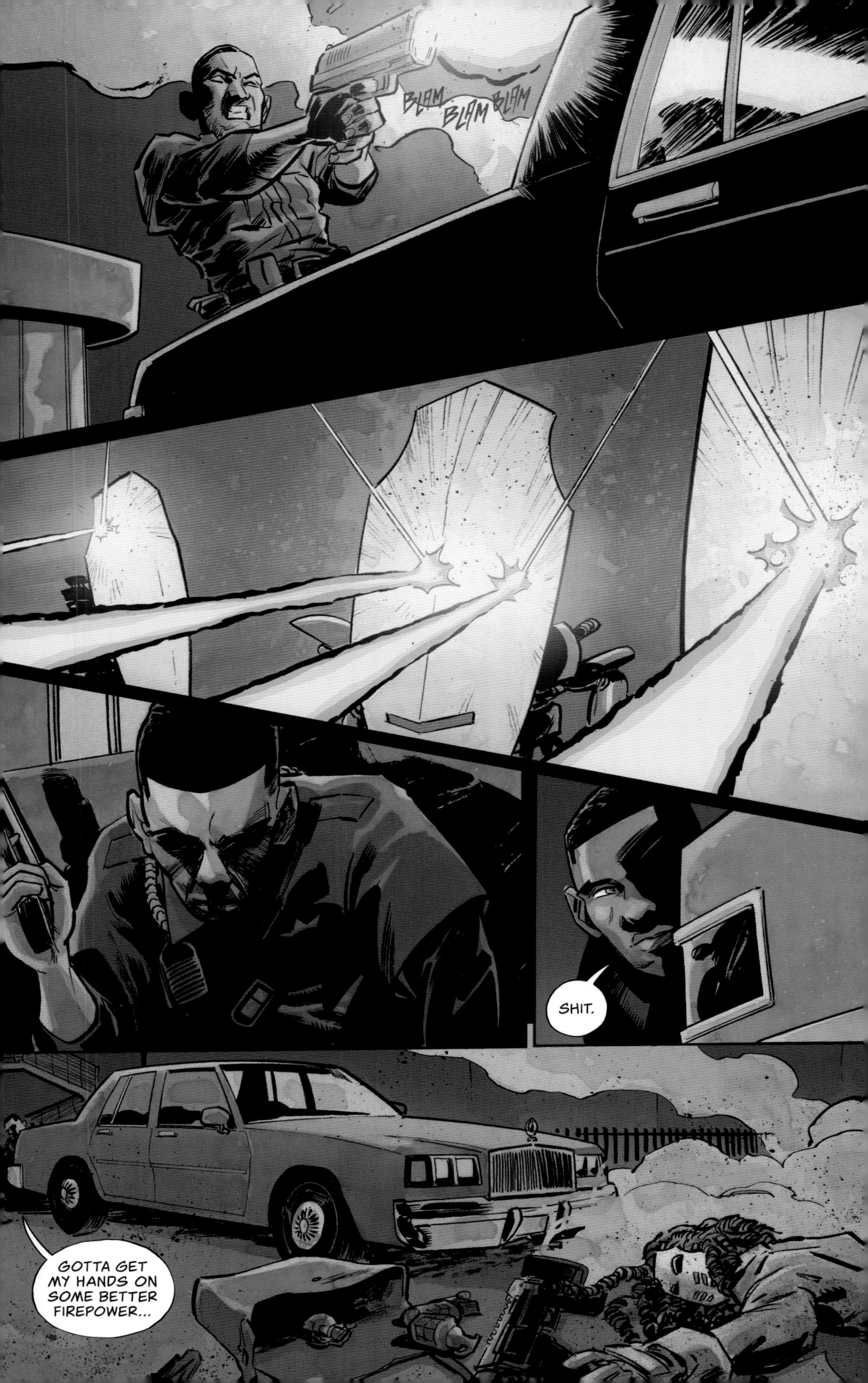
BLAM
BLAM
BLAM
SHIT.
GOTTA GET MY HANDS ON SOME BETTER FIREPOWER...

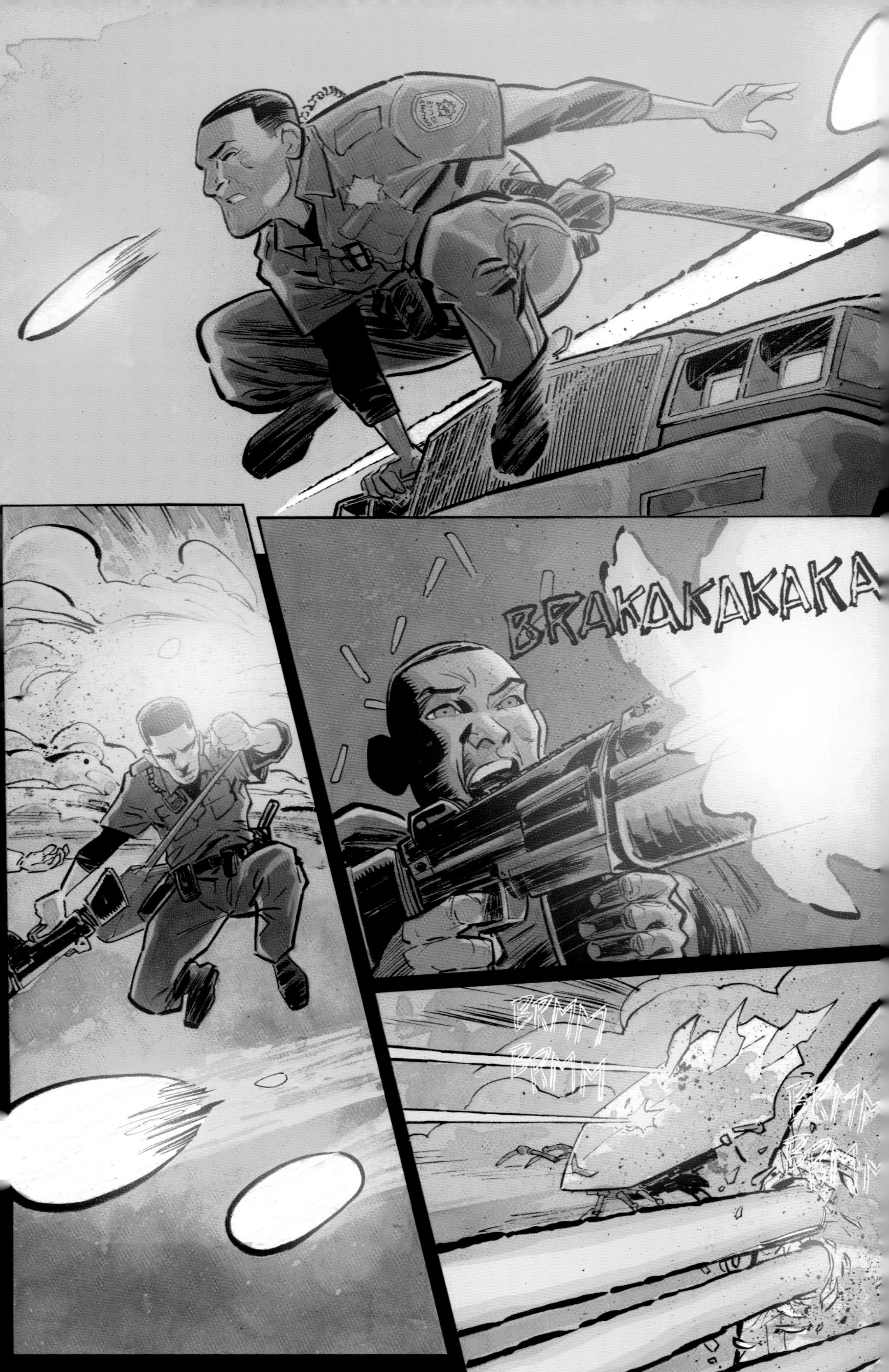
BRAKAKAKAKA
BRMM
BRMM
BRMM
BRMM

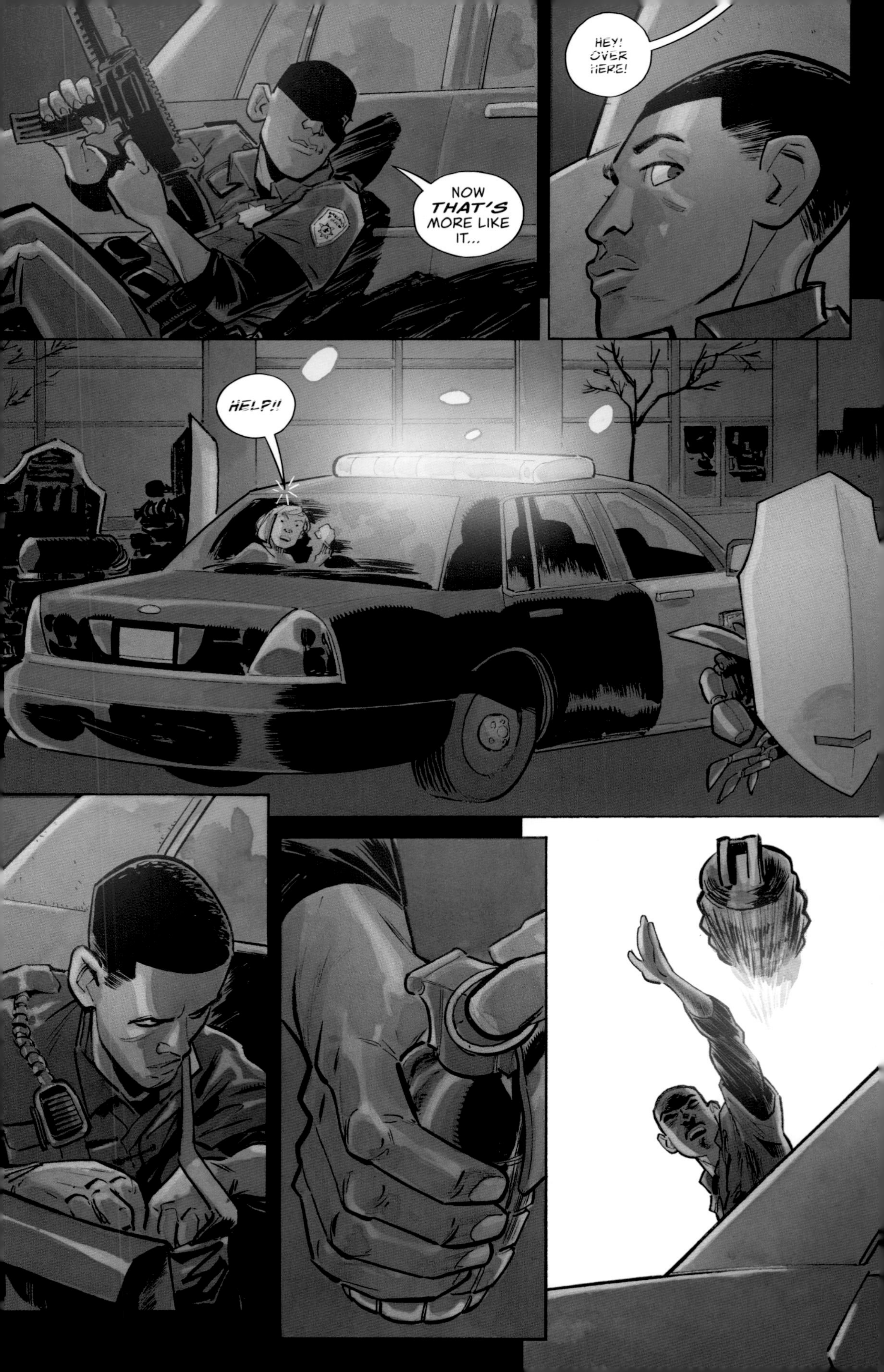
NOW THAT'S MORE LIKE IT...
HEY! OVER HERE!
HELP!!

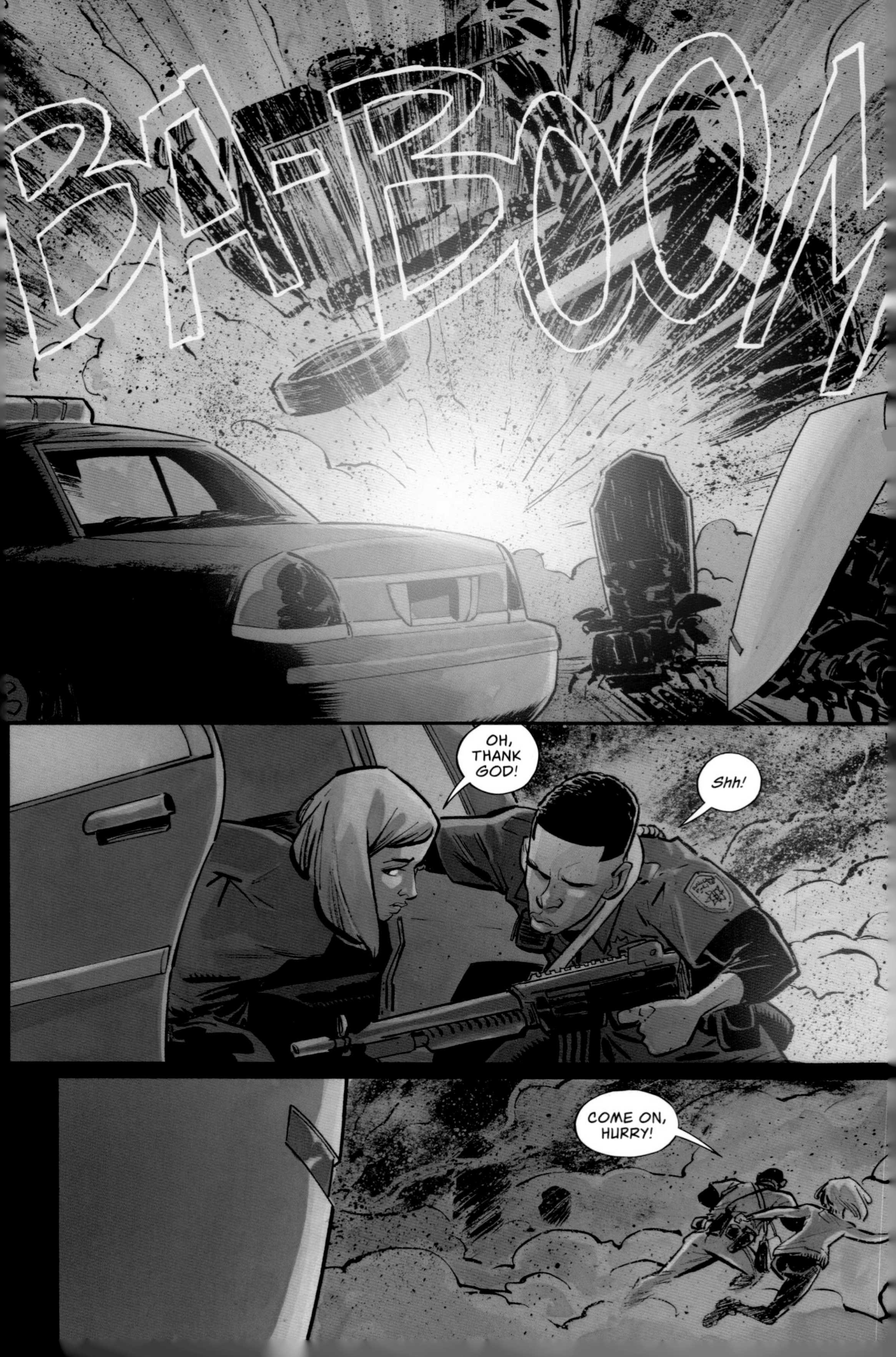
BA-BOOM
OH, THANK GOD!
Shh!
COME ON, HURRY!

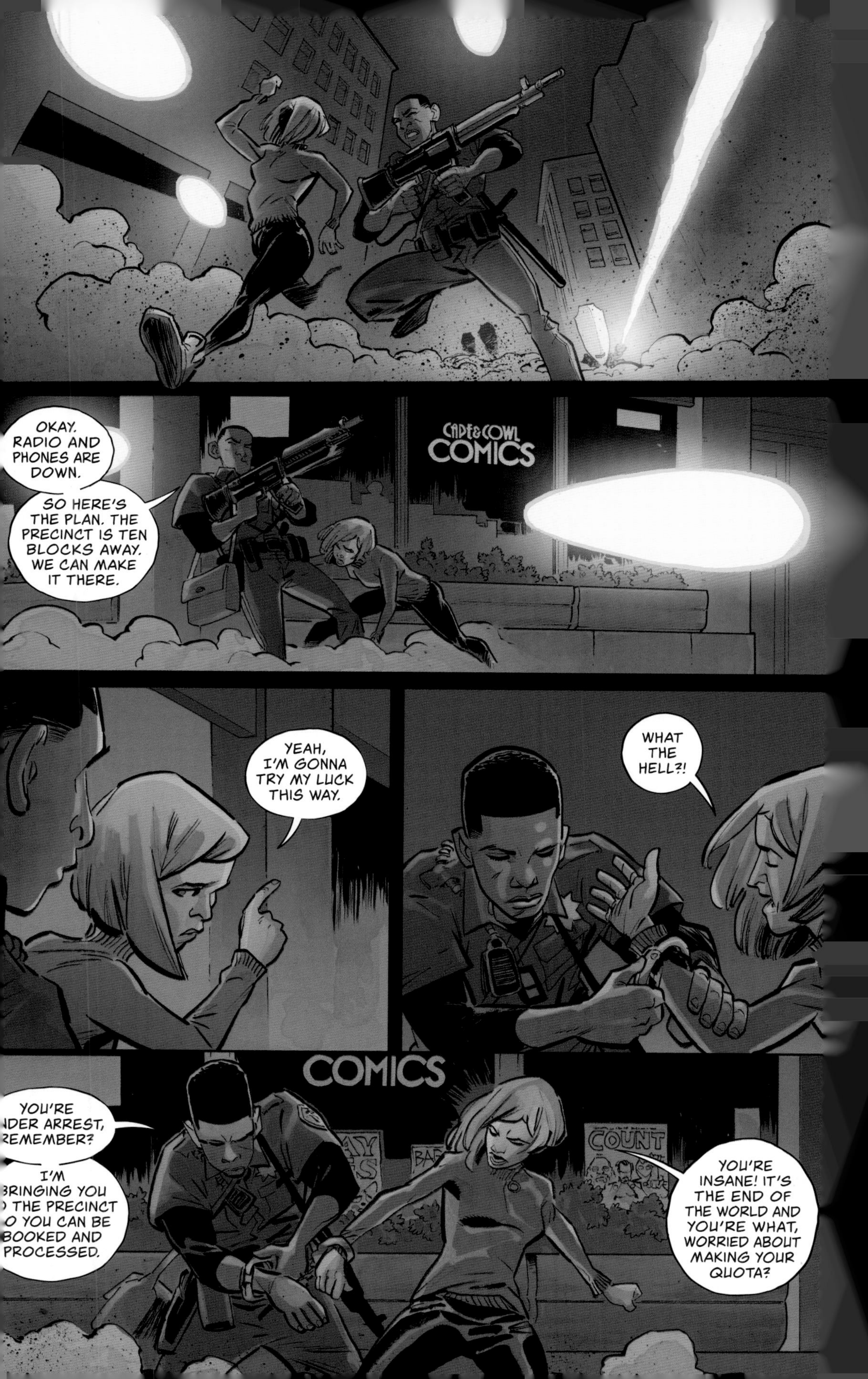

CAPE & COWL COMICS
OKAY. RADIO AND PHONES ARE DOWN.
SO HERE'S THE PLAN. THE PRECINCT IS TEN BLOCKS AWAY. WE CAN MAKE IT THERE.
YEAH, I'M GONNA TRY MY LUCK THIS WAY.
WHAT THE HELL?!
COMICS
YOU'RE
NDER ARREST,
REMEMBER?
I'M
BRINGING YOU
THE PRECINCT
O YOU CAN BE
BOOKED AND
PROCESSED.
COUNT
YOU'RE INSANE! IT'S THE END OF THE WORLD AND YOU'RE WHAT, WORRIED ABOUT MAKING YOUR QUOTA?

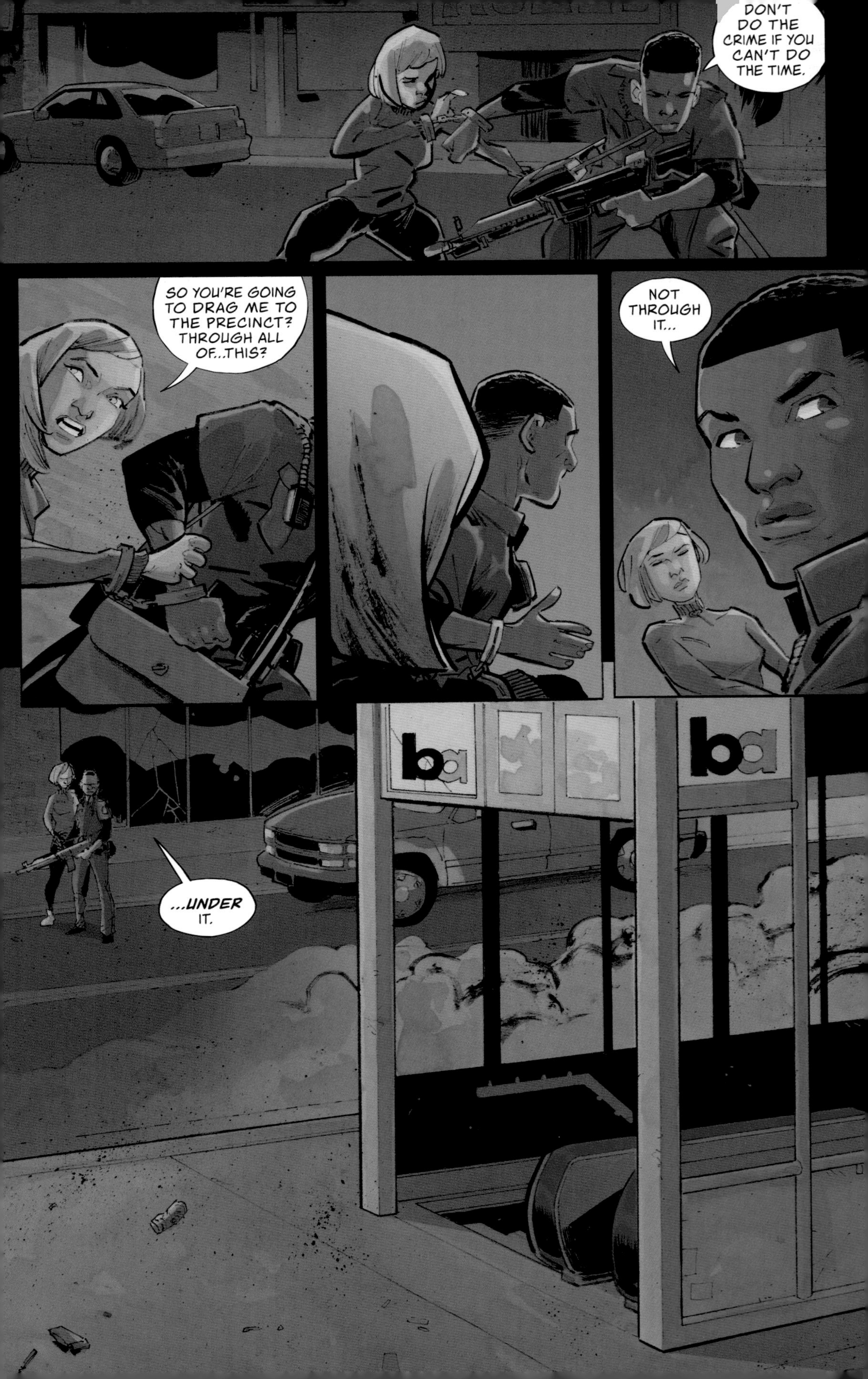
DON'T DO THE CRIME IF YOU CAN'T DO THE TIME.
SO YOU'RE GOING TO DRAG ME TO THE PRECINCT? THROUGH ALL OF...THIS?
NOT THROUGH IT...
...UNDER IT.
ba
ba

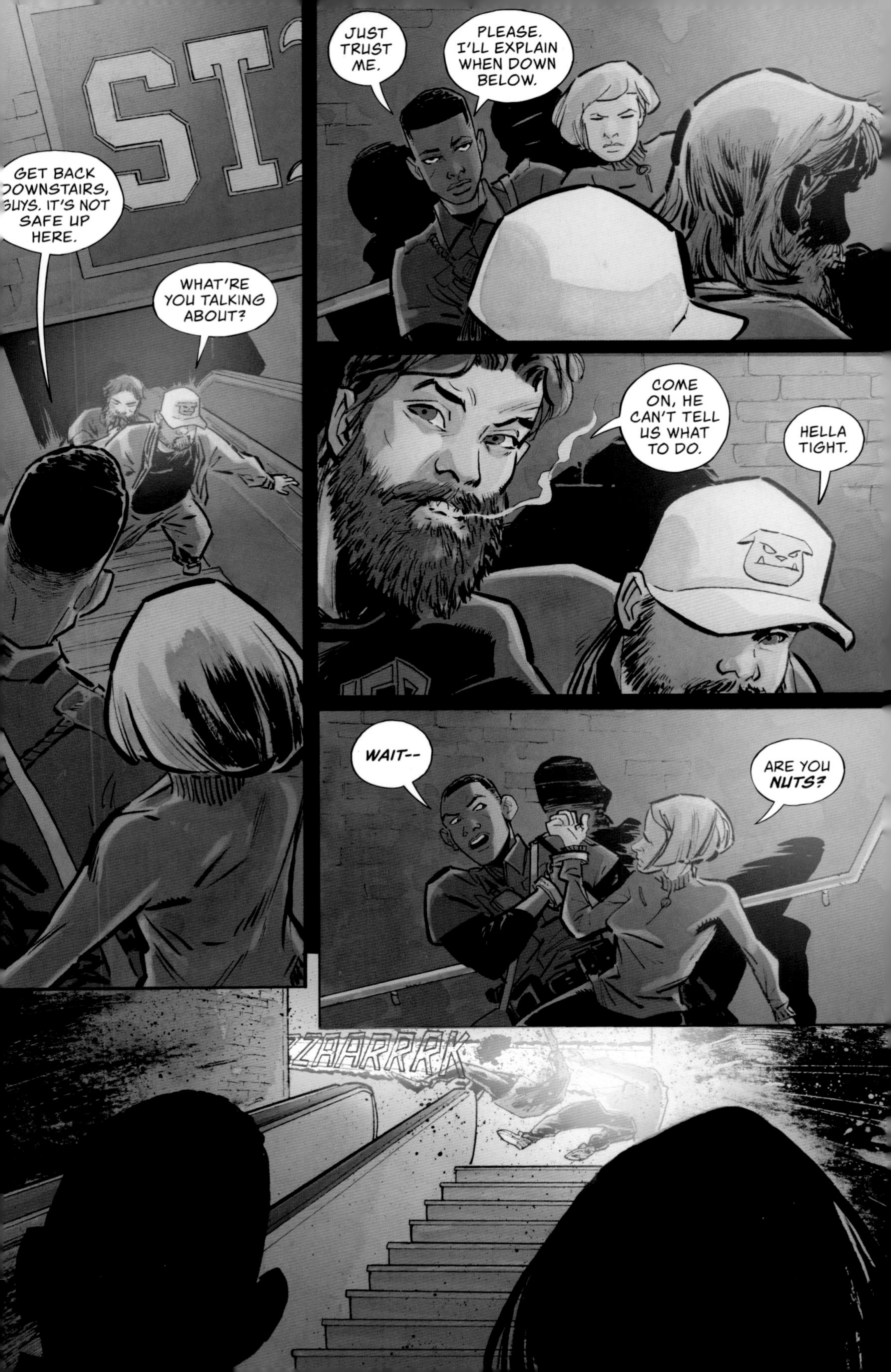
GET BACK DOWNSTAIRS, GUYS. IT'S NOT SAFE UP HERE.
WHAT'RE YOU TALKING ABOUT?
JUST TRUST ME.
PLEASE. I'LL EXPLAIN WHEN DOWN BELOW.
COME ON, HE CAN'T TELL US WHAT TO DO.
HELLA TIGHT.
WAIT--
ARE YOU NUTS?
ZZAARRRRK

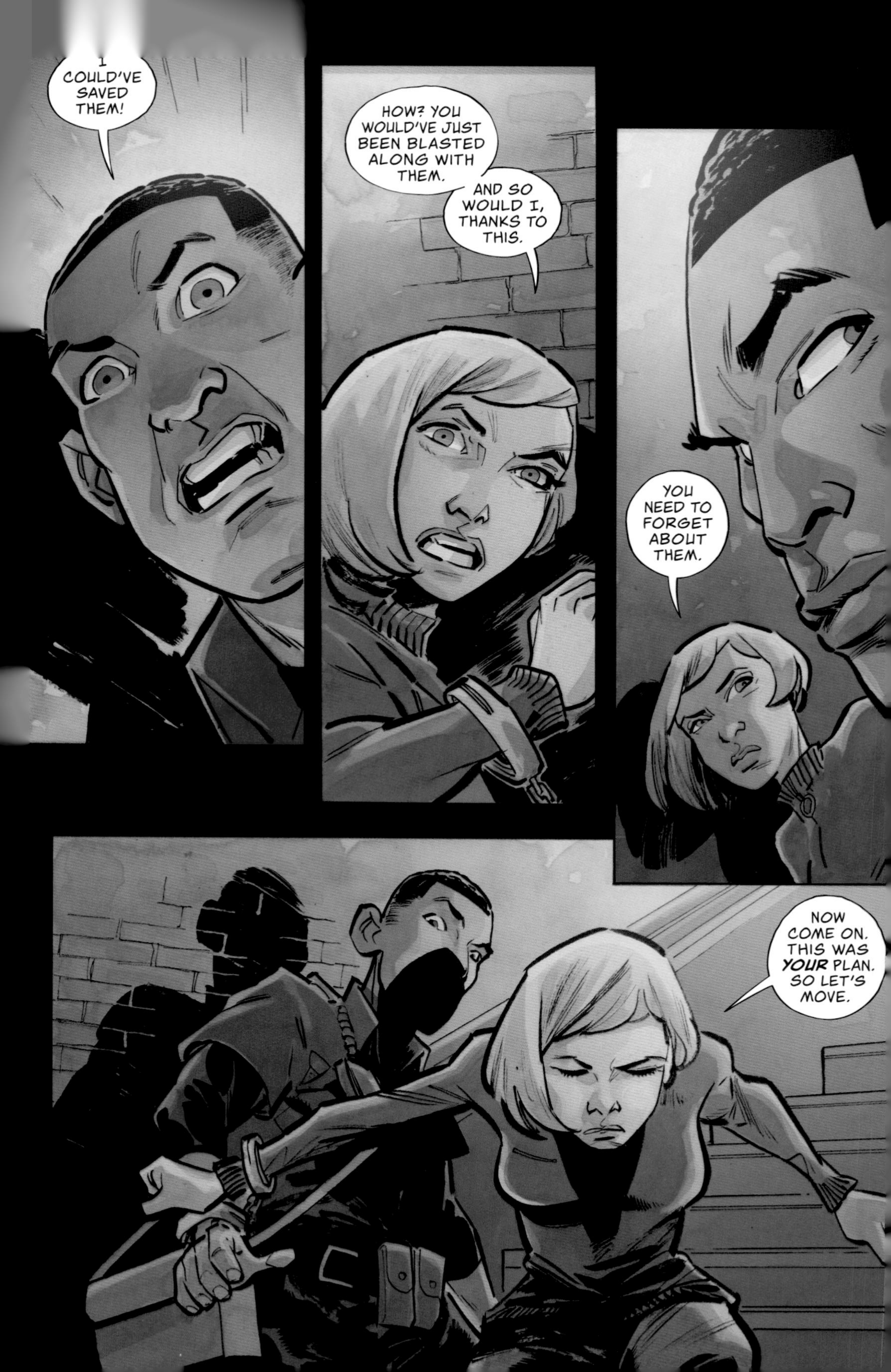
I COULD'VE SAVED THEM!
HOW? YOU WOULD'VE JUST BEEN BLASTED ALONG WITH THEM.
AND SO WOULD I, THANKS TO THIS.
YOU NEED TO FORGET ABOUT THEM.
NOW COME ON. THIS WAS YOUR PLAN. SO LET'S MOVE.

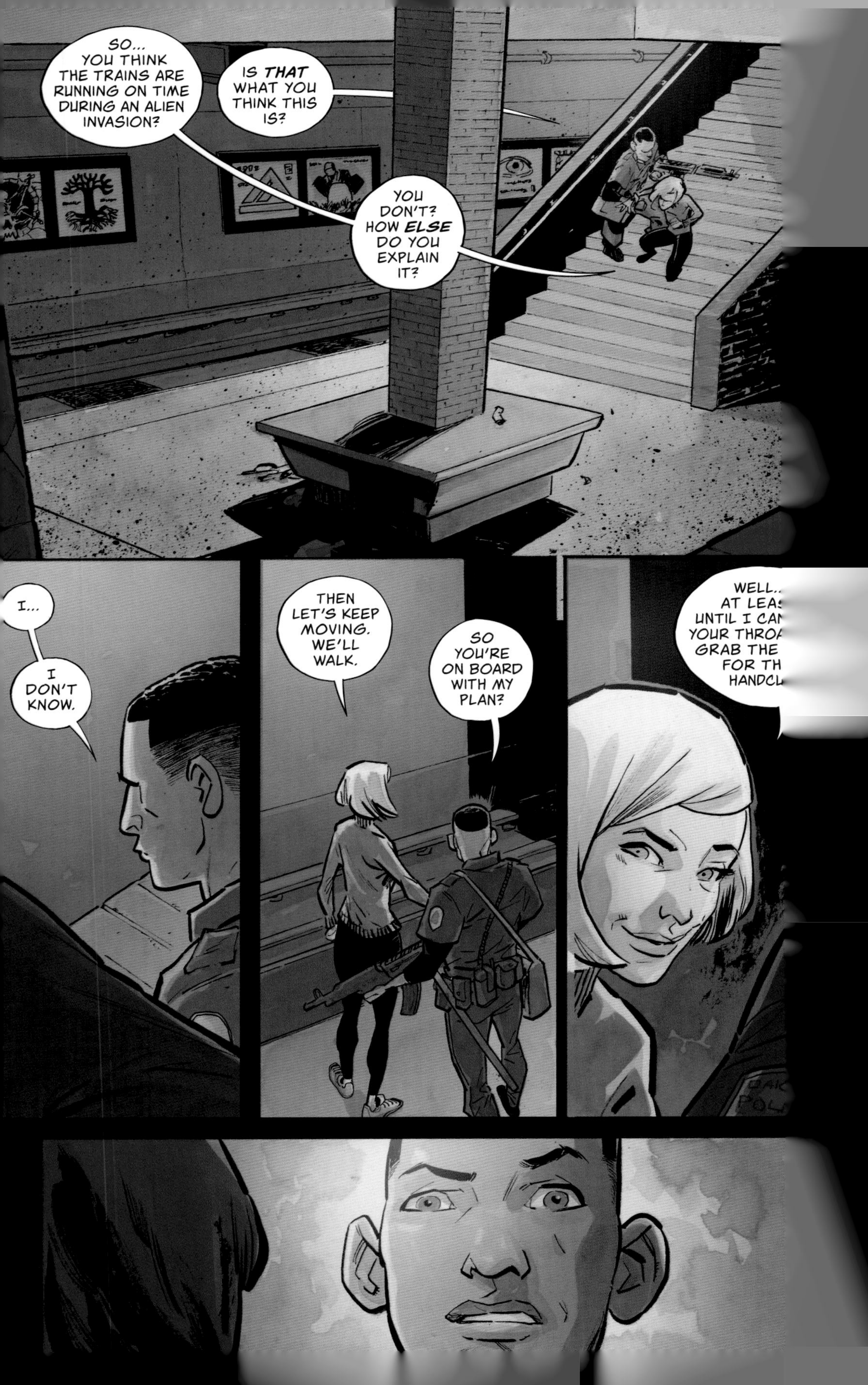
SO... YOU THINK THE TRAINS ARE RUNNING ON TIME DURING AN ALIEN INVASION?
IS THAT WHAT YOU THINK THIS IS?
YOU DON'T? HOW ELSE DO YOU EXPLAIN IT?
I...
I DON'T KNOW.
THEN LET'S KEEP MOVING. WE'LL WALK.
SO YOU'RE ON BOARD WITH MY PLAN?
WELL.. AT LEAS UNTIL I CAN YOUR THROA GRAB THE FOR TH HANDCL

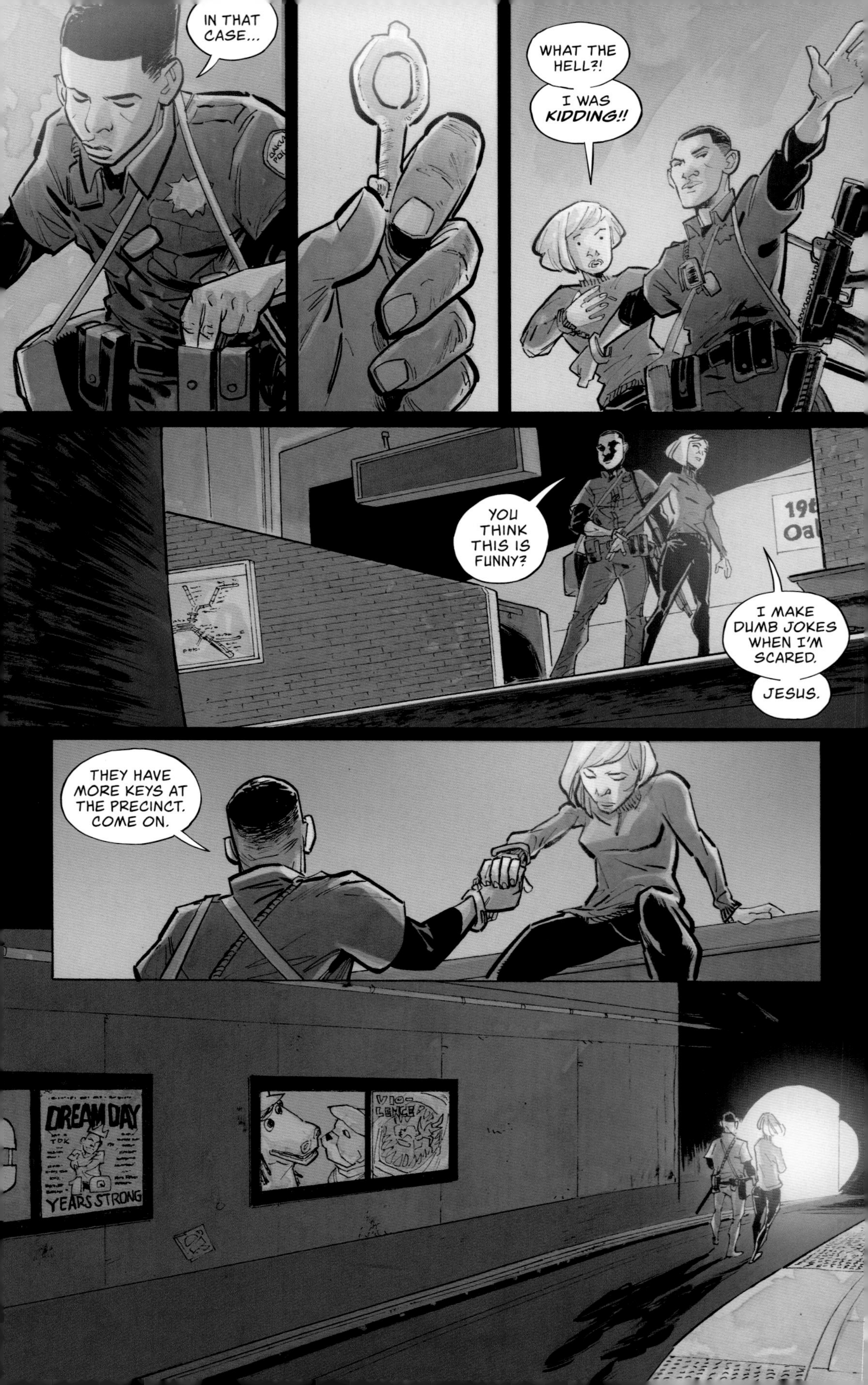
IN THAT CASE...
WHAT THE HELL?!
I WAS KIDDING!!
YOU THINK THIS IS FUNNY?
19t Oal
I MAKE DUMB JOKES WHEN I'M SCARED.
JESUS.
THEY HAVE MORE KEYS AT THE PRECINCT. COME ON.
DREAM DAY
YEARS STRONG
VIO-LENCE?

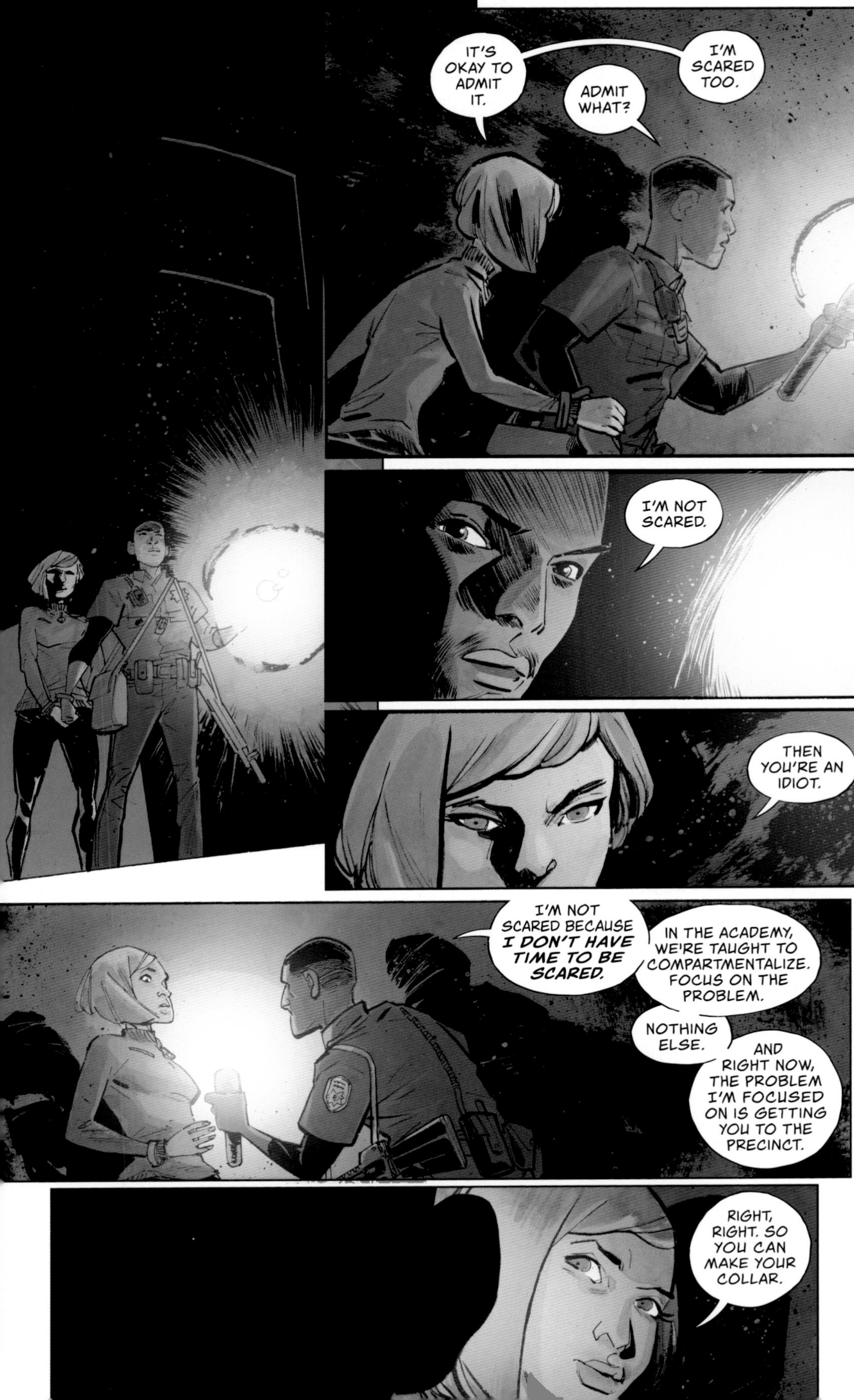
IT'S OKAY TO ADMIT IT.
ADMIT WHAT?
I'M SCARED TOO.
I'M NOT SCARED.
THEN YOU'RE AN IDIOT.
I'M NOT SCARED BECAUSE *I DON'T HAVE TIME TO BE SCARED.*
IN THE ACADEMY, WE'RE TAUGHT TO COMPARTMENTALIZE. FOCUS ON THE PROBLEM.
NOTHING ELSE.
AND RIGHT NOW, THE PROBLEM I'M FOCUSED ON IS GETTING YOU TO THE PRECINCT.
RIGHT, RIGHT. SO YOU CAN MAKE YOUR COLLAR.

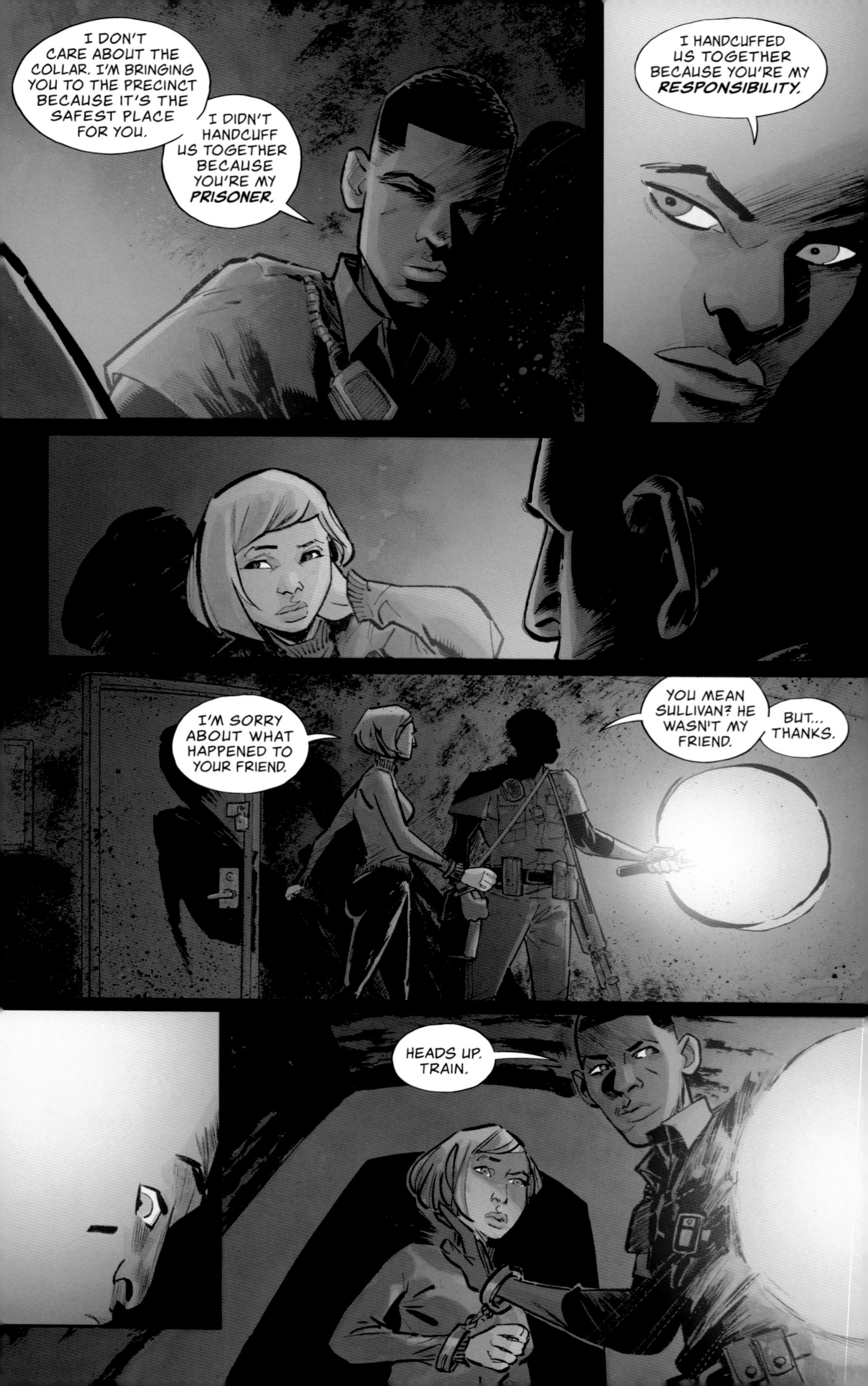
I DON'T CARE ABOUT THE COLLAR. I'M BRINGING YOU TO THE PRECINCT BECAUSE IT'S THE SAFEST PLACE FOR YOU.
I DIDN'T HANDCUFF US TOGETHER BECAUSE YOU'RE MY PRISONER.
I HANDCUFFED US TOGETHER BECAUSE YOU'RE MY RESPONSIBILITY.
I'M SORRY ABOUT WHAT HAPPENED TO YOUR FRIEND.
YOU MEAN SULLIVAN? HE WASN'T MY FRIEND.
BUT... THANKS.
HEADS UP. TRAIN.

THAT'S NOT A TRAIN...

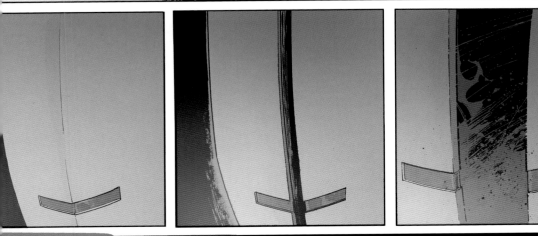

HOLY SHIT, THEY'RE WEARING ARMOR!

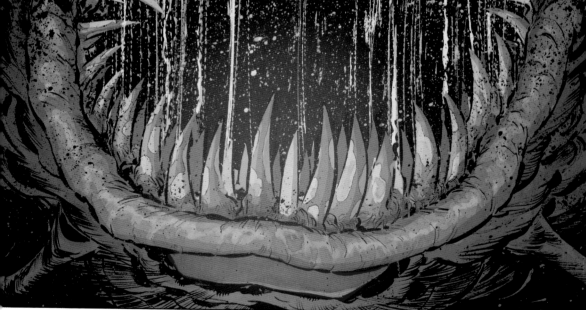

HURRY!!

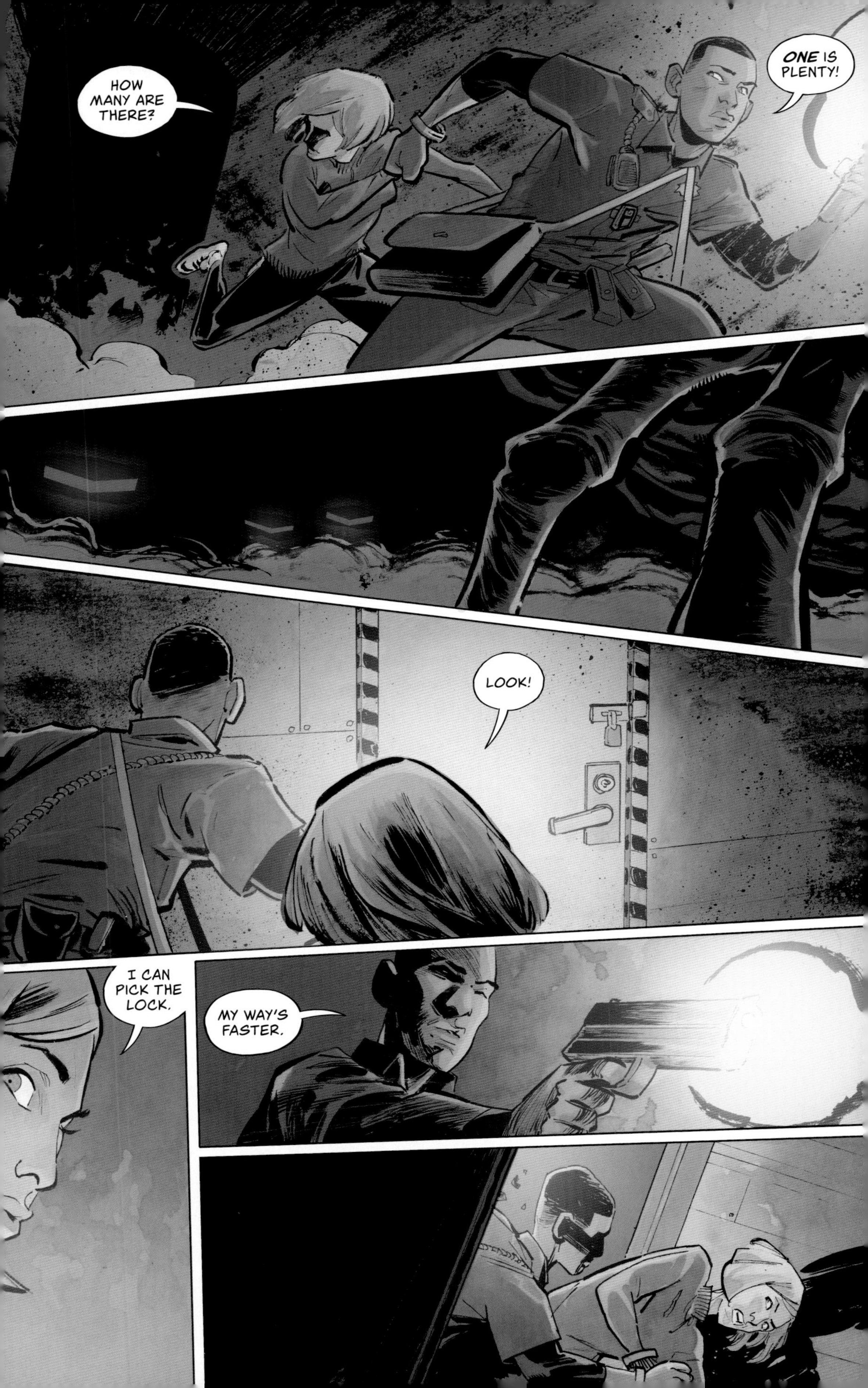
HOW MANY ARE THERE?
ONE IS PLENTY!
LOOK!
I CAN PICK THE LOCK.
MY WAY'S FASTER.

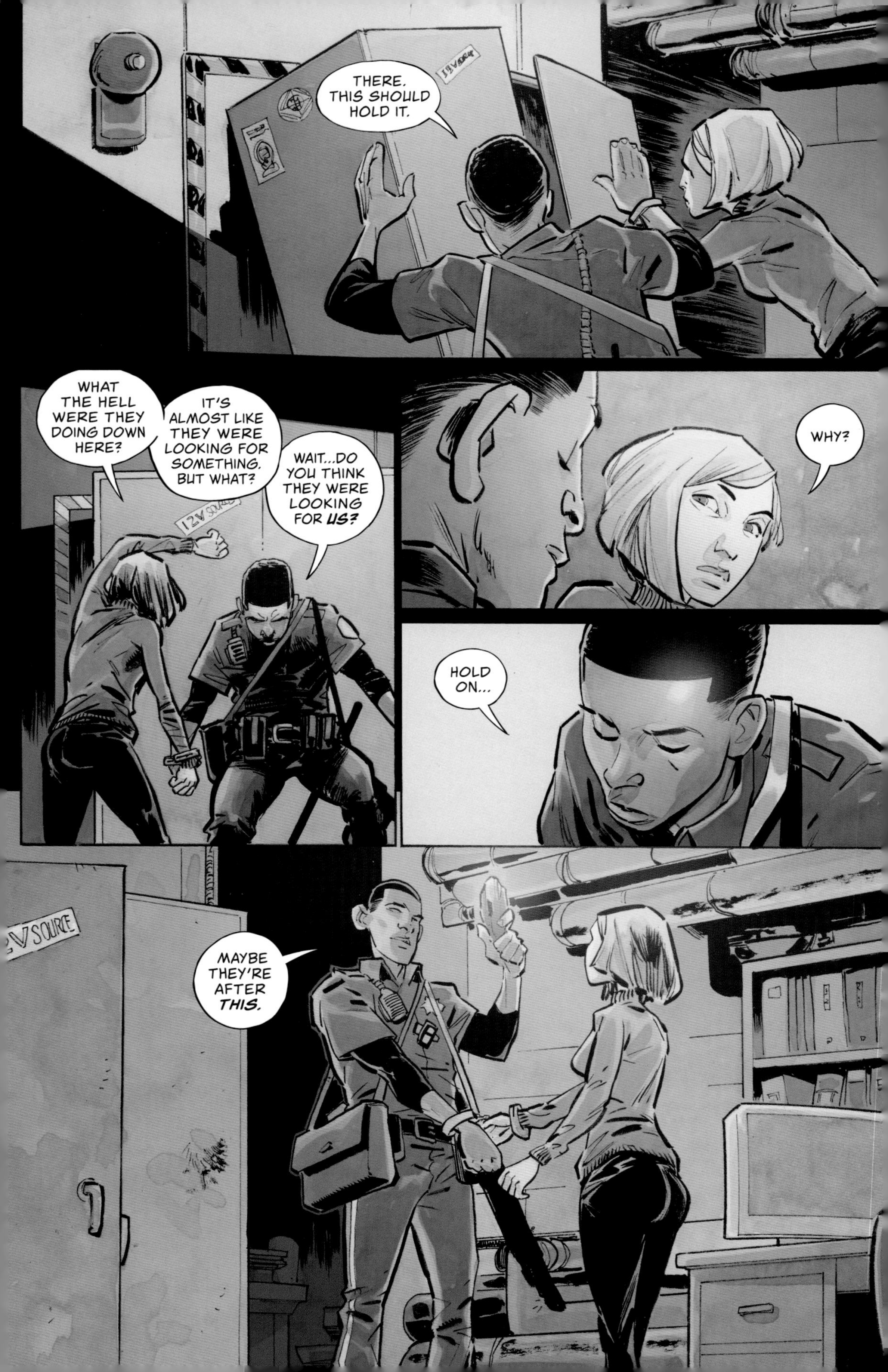
THERE. THIS SHOULD HOLD IT.
WHAT THE HELL WERE THEY DOING DOWN HERE?
IT'S ALMOST LIKE THEY WERE LOOKING FOR SOMETHING. BUT WHAT?
WAIT...DO YOU THINK THEY WERE LOOKING FOR *US?*
WHY?
HOLD ON...
MAYBE THEY'RE AFTER *THIS.*

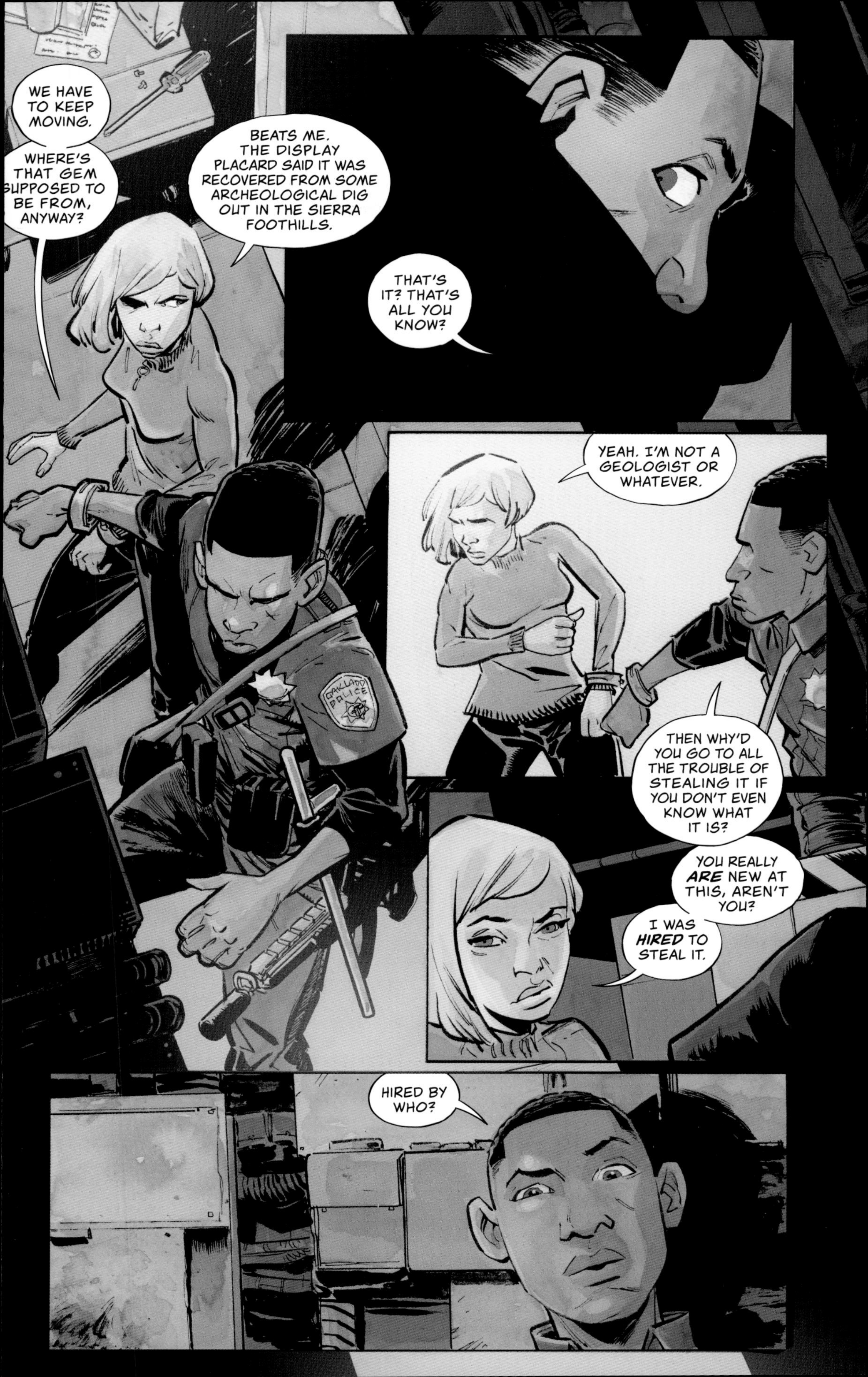
WE HAVE TO KEEP MOVING.
WHERE'S THAT GEM SUPPOSED TO BE FROM, ANYWAY?
BEATS ME. THE DISPLAY PLACARD SAID IT WAS RECOVERED FROM SOME ARCHEOLOGICAL DIG OUT IN THE SIERRA FOOTHILLS.
THAT'S IT? THAT'S ALL YOU KNOW?
YEAH. I'M NOT A GEOLOGIST OR WHATEVER.
THEN WHY'D YOU GO TO ALL THE TROUBLE OF STEALING IT IF YOU DON'T EVEN KNOW WHAT IT IS?
YOU REALLY ARE NEW AT THIS, AREN'T YOU?
I WAS HIRED TO STEAL IT.
HIRED BY WHO?
OAKLAND POLICE

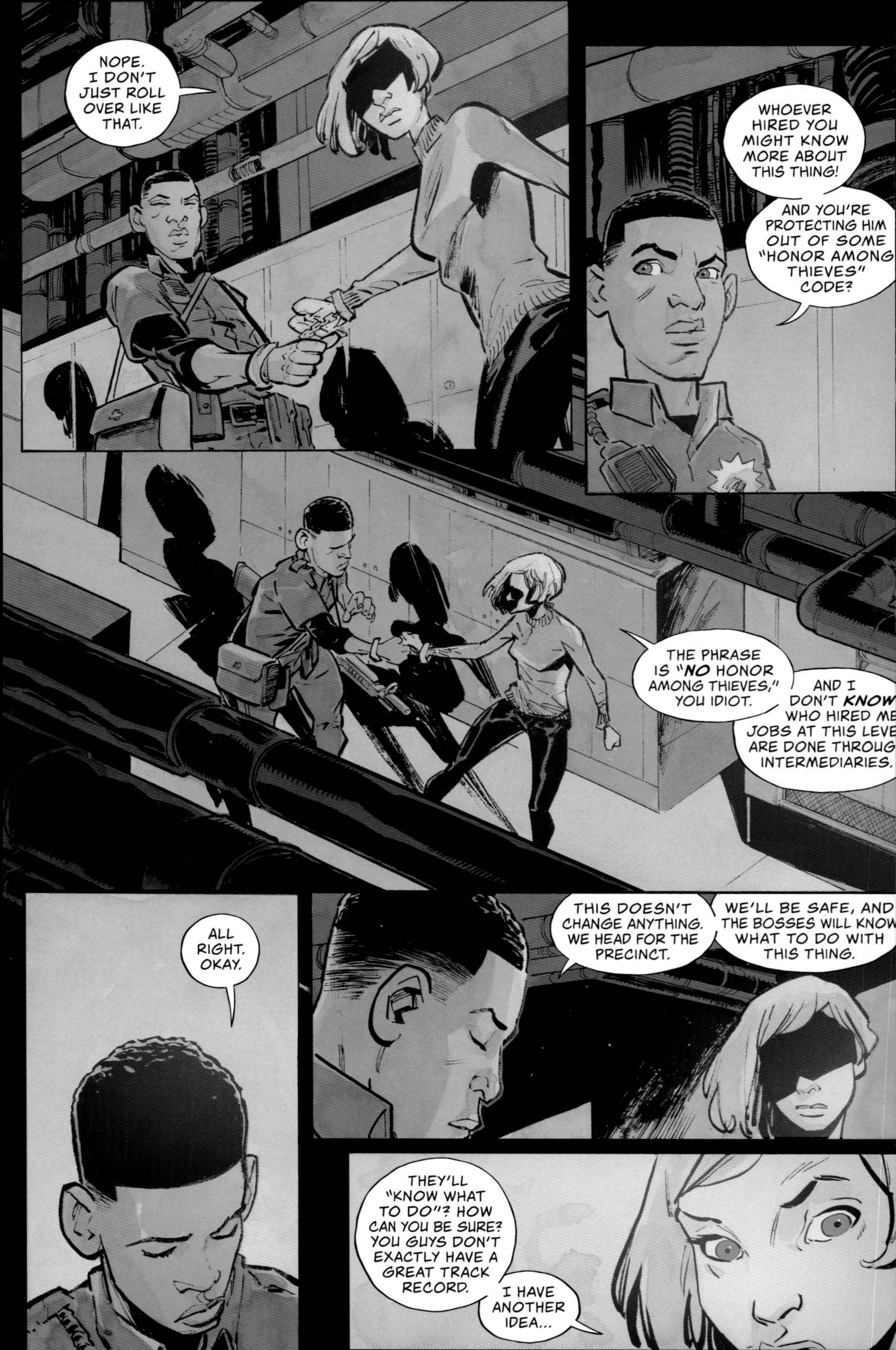
NOPE. I DON'T JUST ROLL OVER LIKE THAT.
WHOEVER HIRED YOU MIGHT KNOW MORE ABOUT THIS THING!
AND YOU'RE PROTECTING HIM OUT OF SOME "HONOR AMONG THIEVES" CODE?
THE PHRASE IS "NO HONOR AMONG THIEVES," YOU IDIOT.
AND I DON'T KNOW WHO HIRED ME. JOBS AT THIS LEVE ARE DONE THROUG INTERMEDIARIES.
ALL RIGHT. OKAY.
THIS DOESN'T CHANGE ANYTHING. WE HEAD FOR THE PRECINCT.
WE'LL BE SAFE, AND THE BOSSES WILL KNOW WHAT TO DO WITH THIS THING.
THEY'LL "KNOW WHAT TO DO"? HOW CAN YOU BE SURE? YOU GUYS DON'T EXACTLY HAVE A GREAT TRACK RECORD.
I HAVE ANOTHER IDEA...

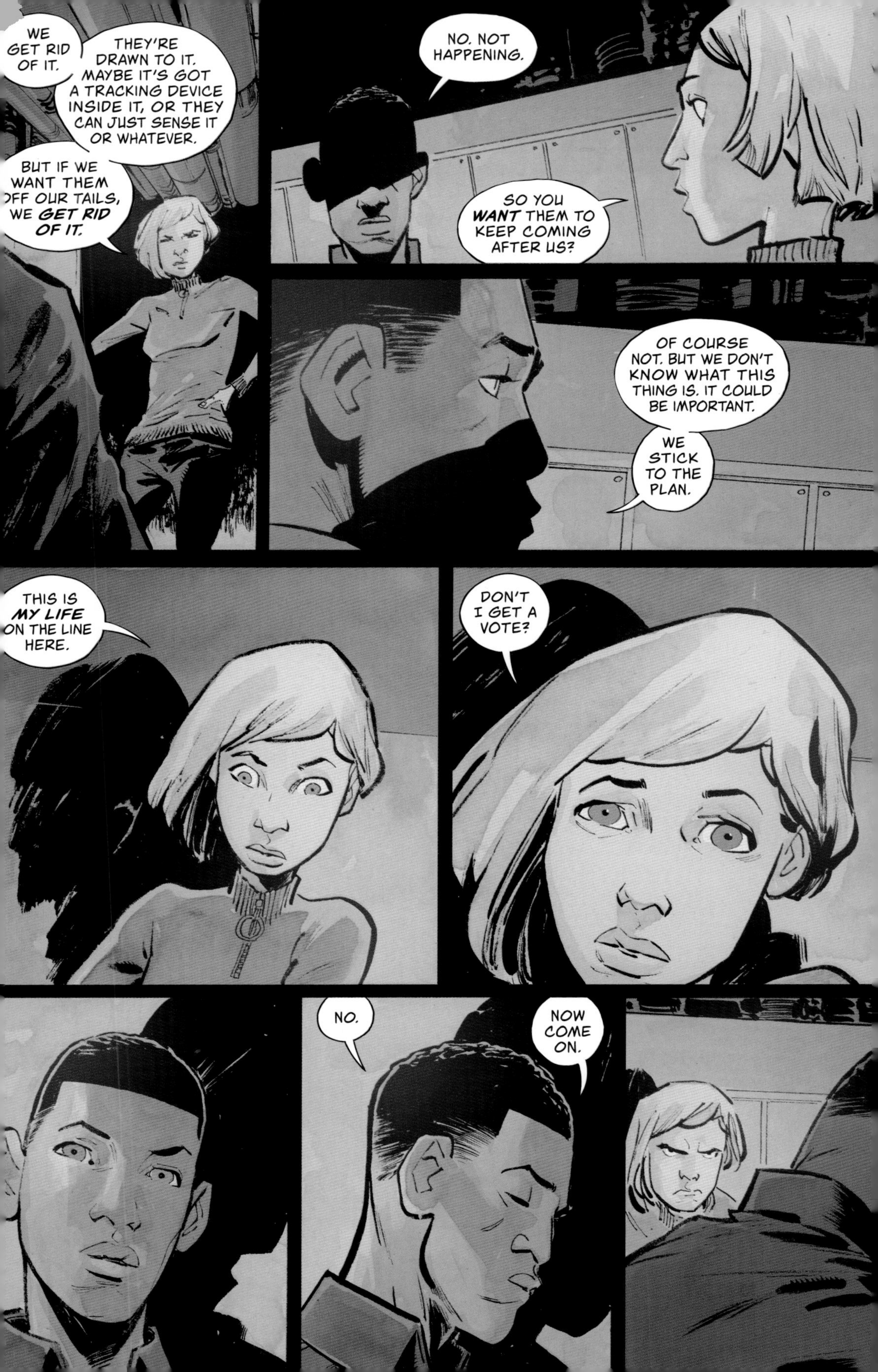
WE GET RID OF IT.
THEY'RE DRAWN TO IT. MAYBE IT'S GOT A TRACKING DEVICE INSIDE IT, OR THEY CAN JUST SENSE IT OR WHATEVER.
BUT IF WE WANT THEM OFF OUR TAILS, WE GET RID OF IT.
NO. NOT HAPPENING.
SO YOU WANT THEM TO KEEP COMING AFTER US?
OF COURSE NOT. BUT WE DON'T KNOW WHAT THIS THING IS. IT COULD BE IMPORTANT.
WE STICK TO THE PLAN.
THIS IS MY LIFE ON THE LINE HERE.
DON'T I GET A VOTE?
NO.
NOW COME ON.

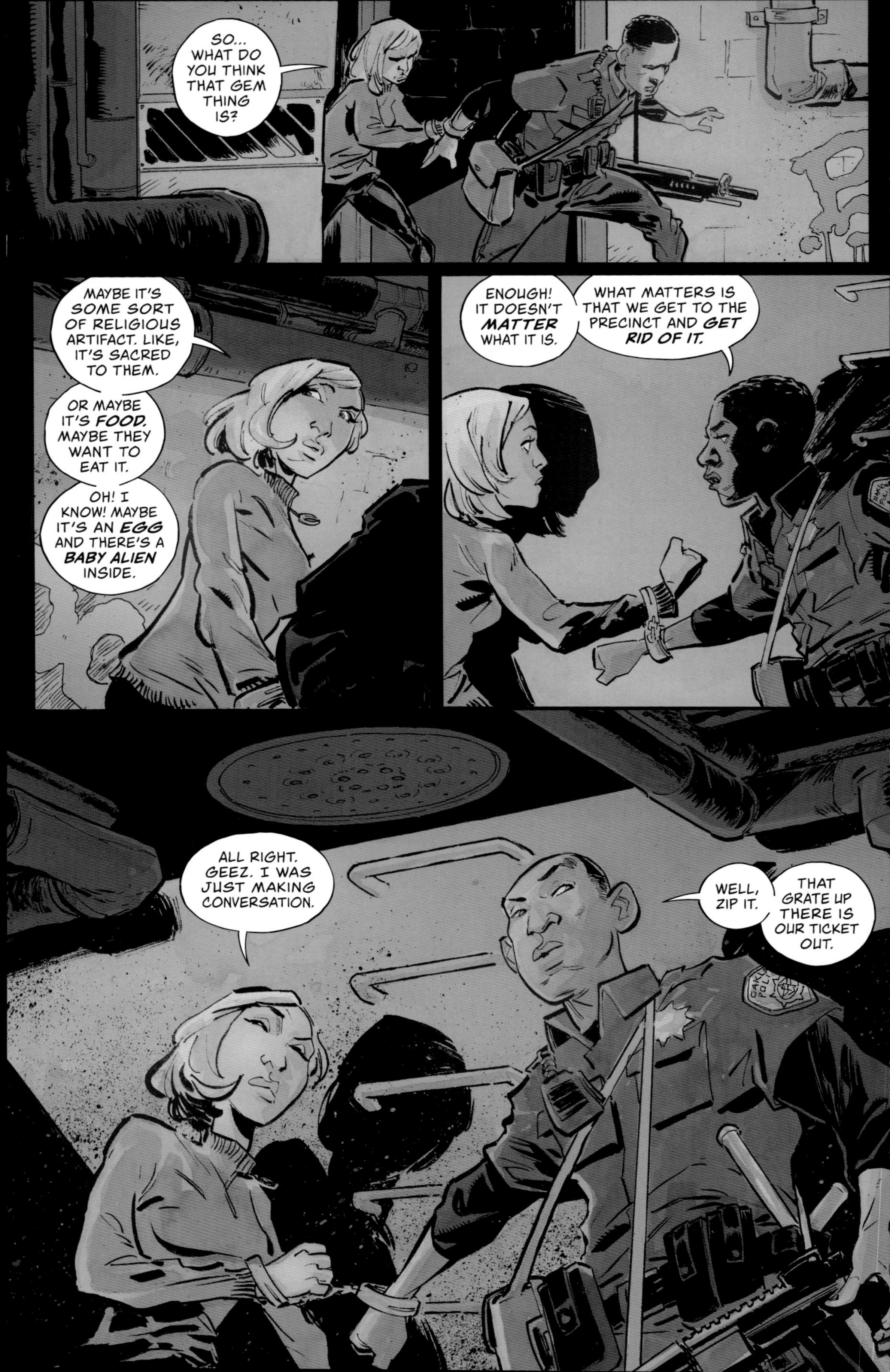
SO... WHAT DO YOU THINK THAT GEM THING IS?
MAYBE IT'S SOME SORT OF RELIGIOUS ARTIFACT. LIKE, IT'S SACRED TO THEM.
OR MAYBE IT'S FOOD. MAYBE THEY WANT TO EAT IT.
OH! I KNOW! MAYBE IT'S AN EGG AND THERE'S A BABY ALIEN INSIDE.
ENOUGH! IT DOESN'T MATTER WHAT IT IS.
WHAT MATTERS IS THAT WE GET TO THE PRECINCT AND GET RID OF IT.
ALL RIGHT. GEEZ. I WAS JUST MAKING CONVERSATION.
WELL, ZIP IT.
THAT GRATE UP THERE IS OUR TICKET OUT.

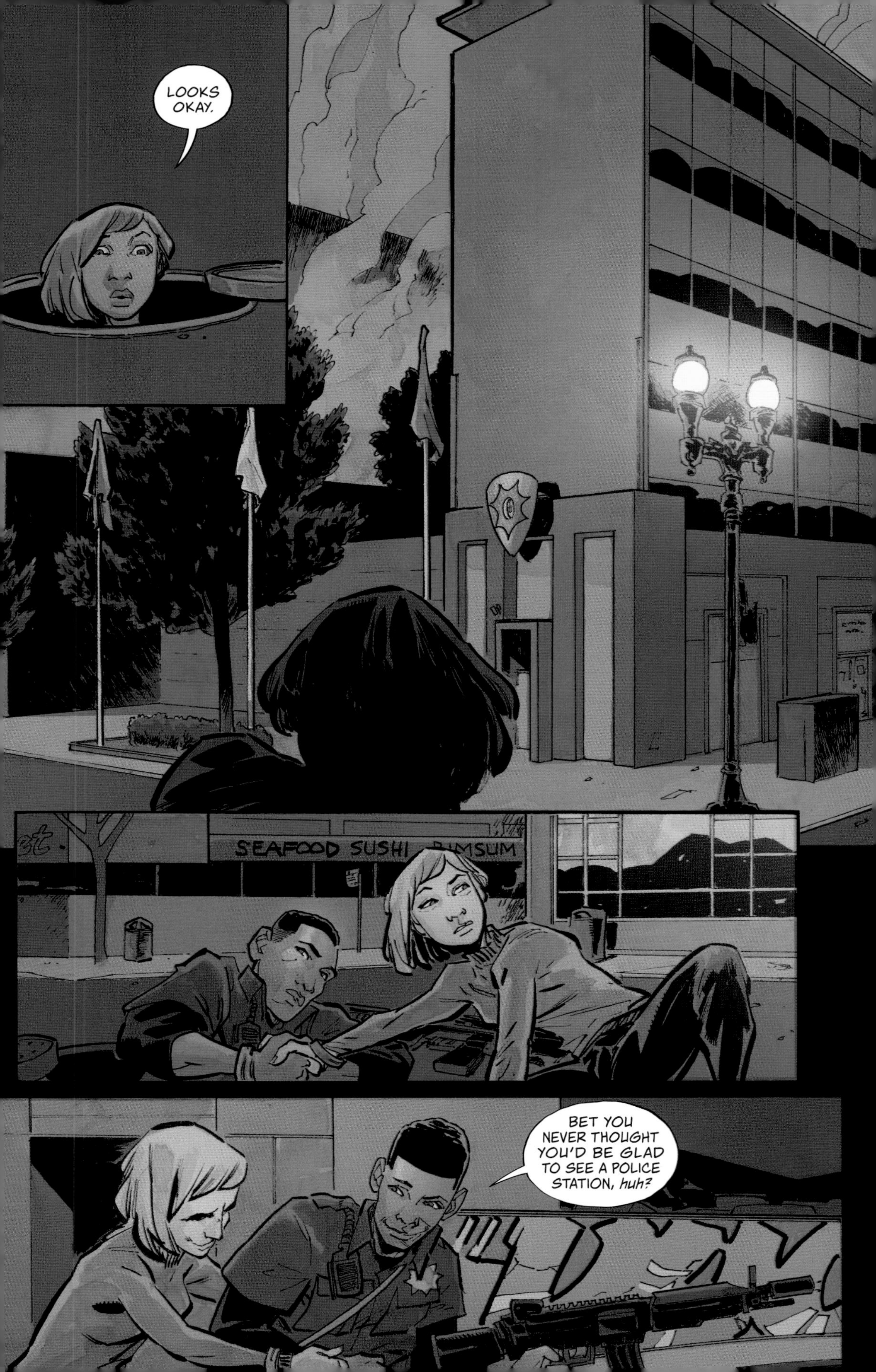
LOOKS OKAY.
SEAFOOD SUSHI DIMSUM
BET YOU NEVER THOUGHT YOU'D BE GLAD TO SEE A POLICE STATION, *huh?*

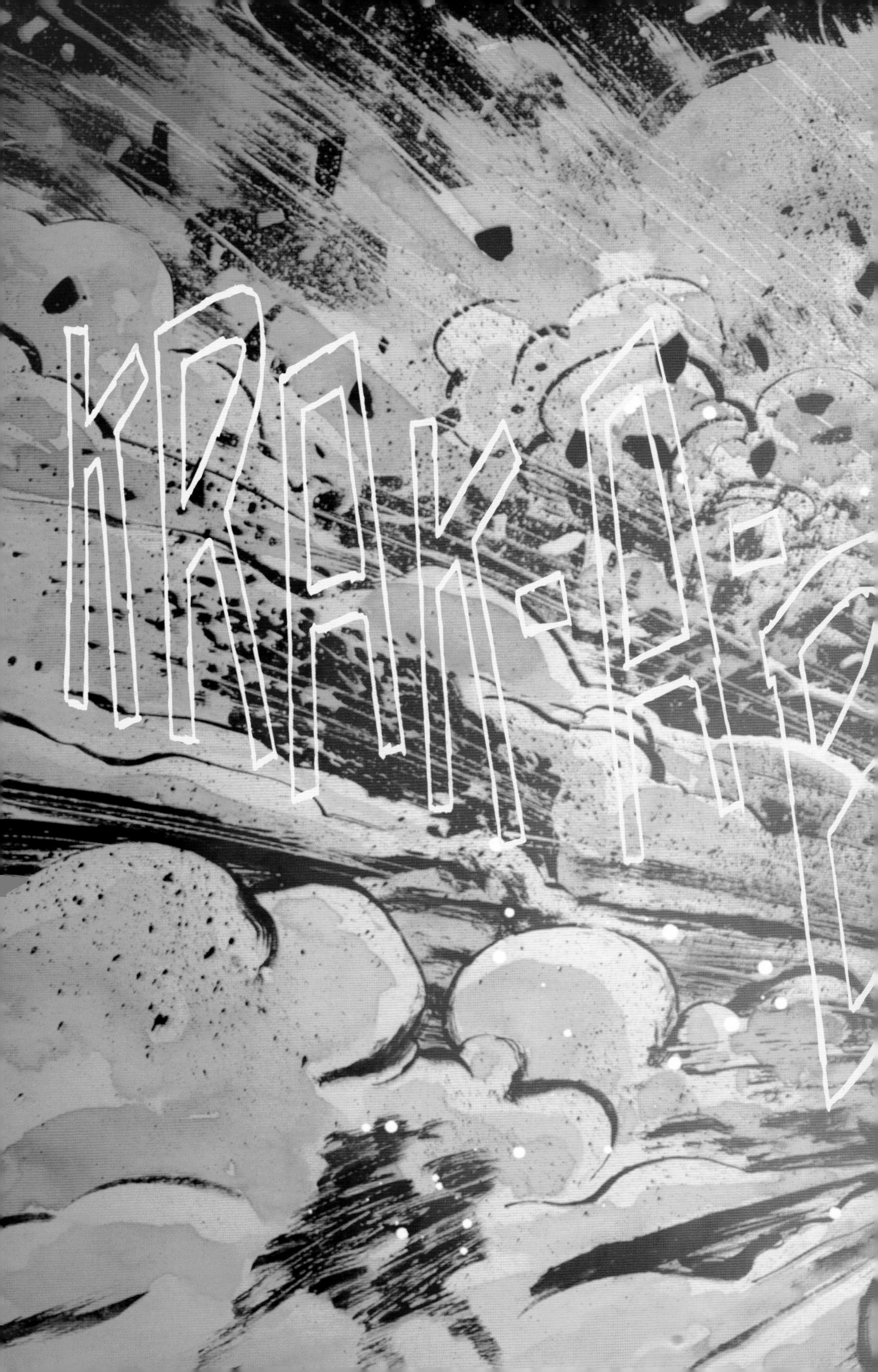
KRAK-A-

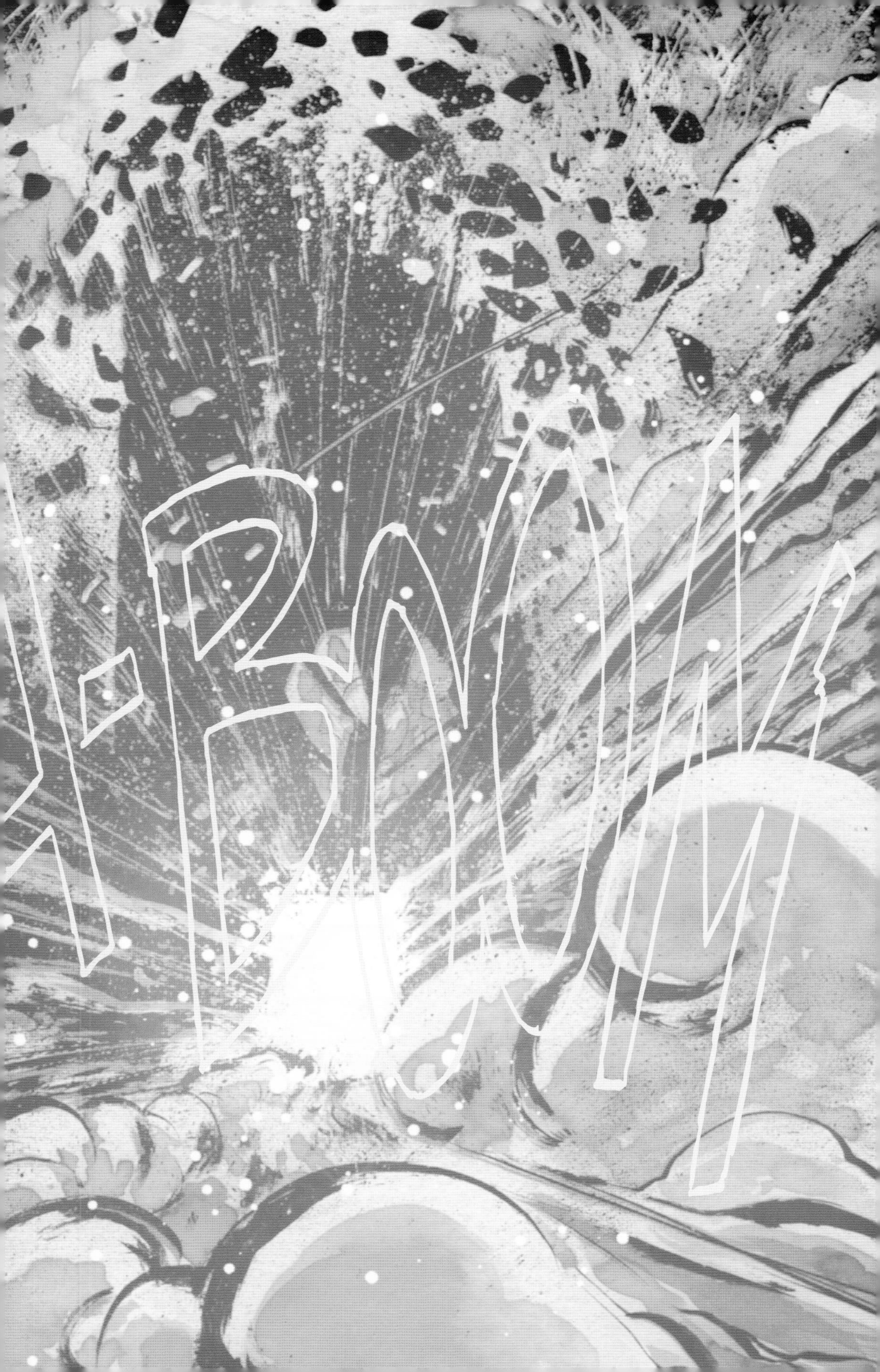

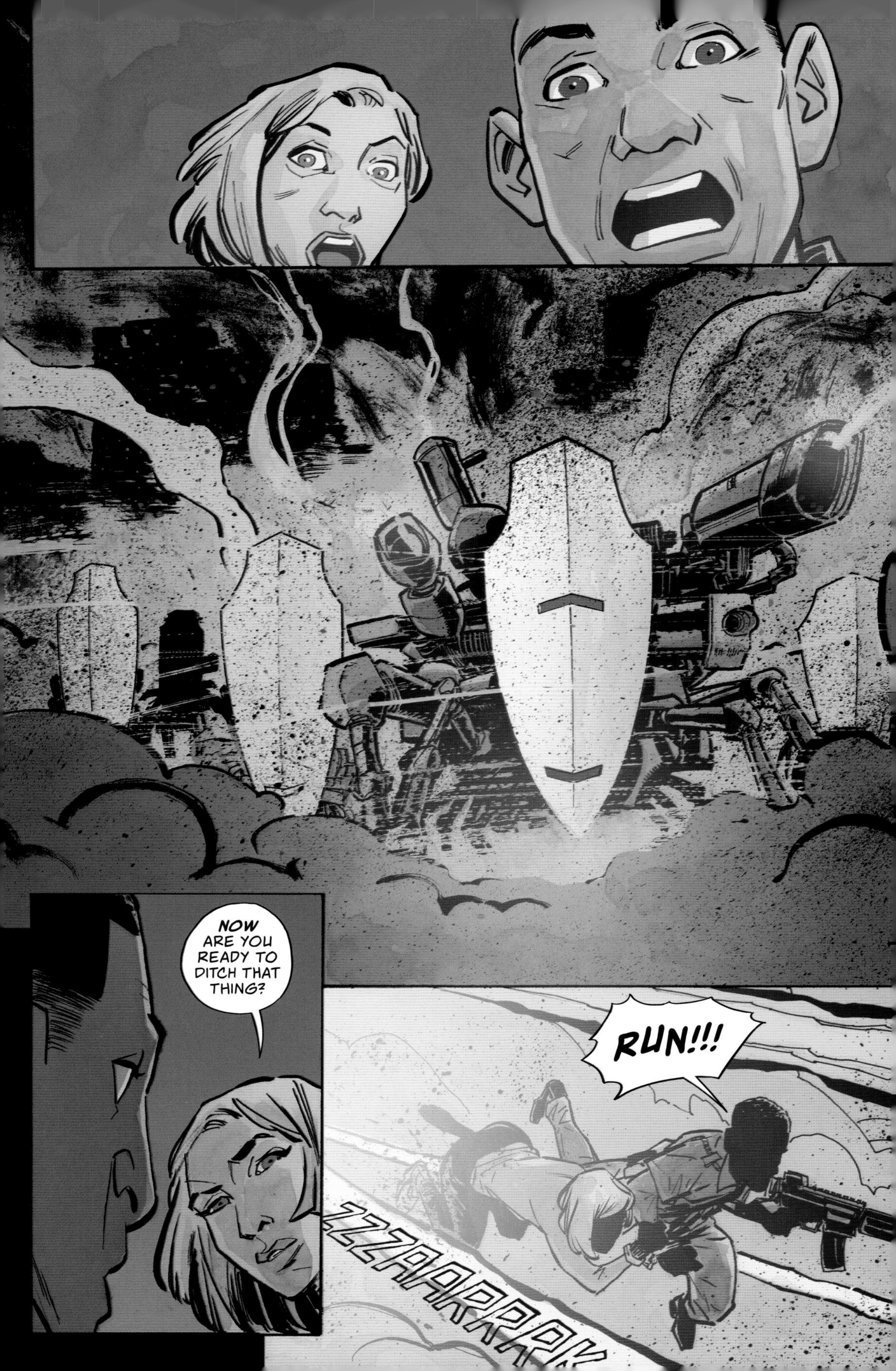
NOW ARE YOU READY TO DITCH THAT THING?
RUN!!!
ZZZARRRRK

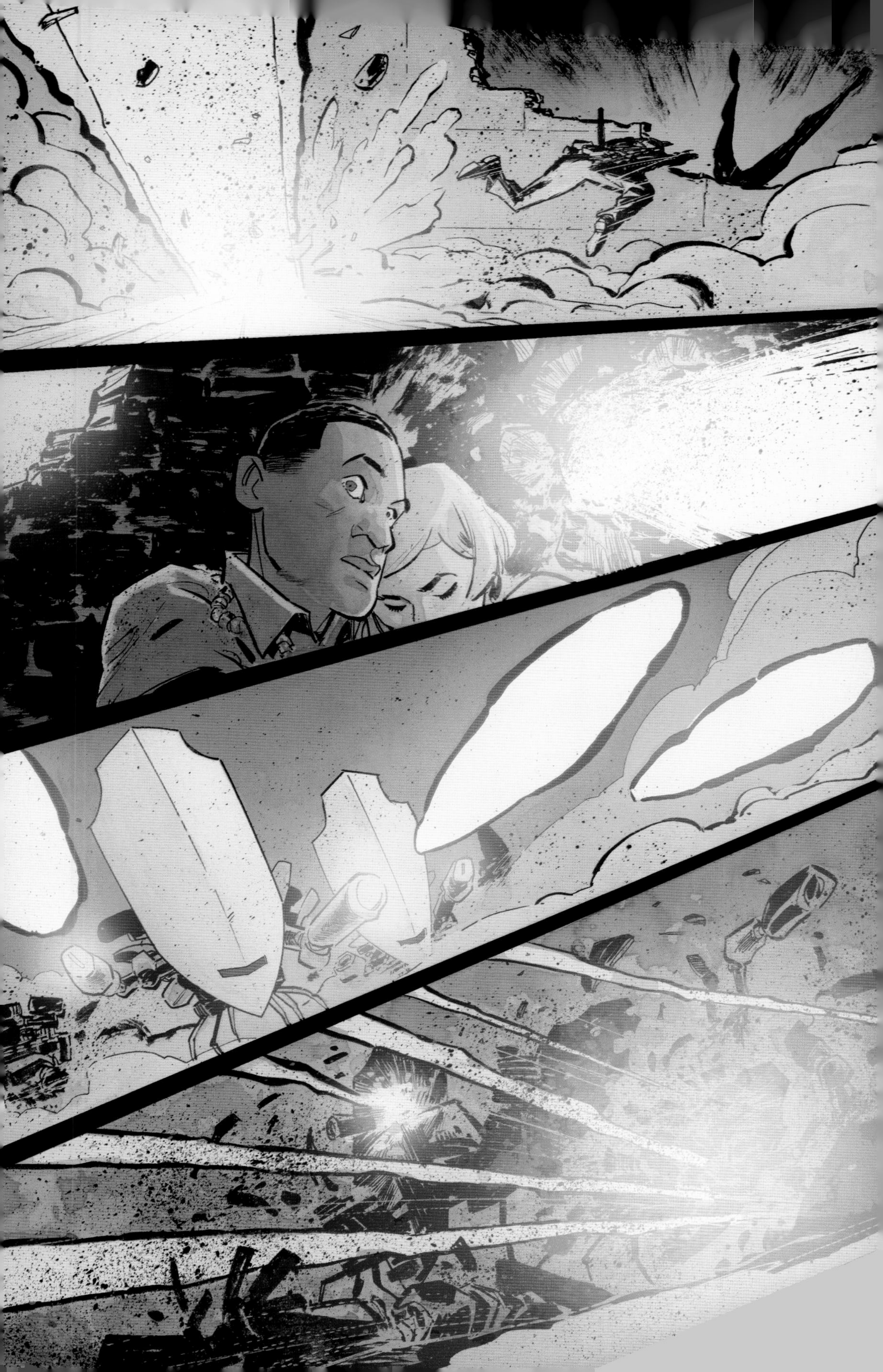

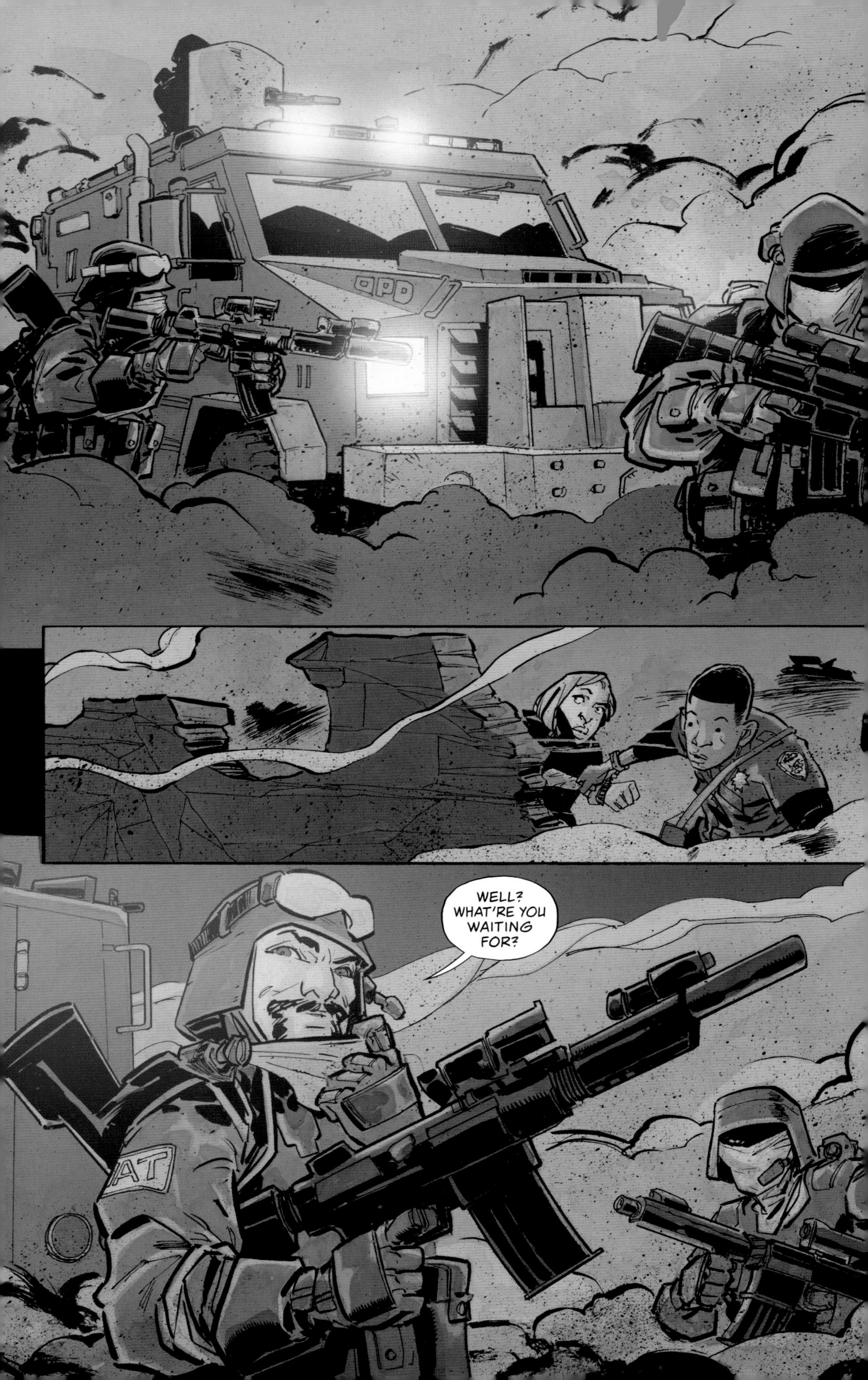
WELL? WHAT'RE YOU WAITING FOR?

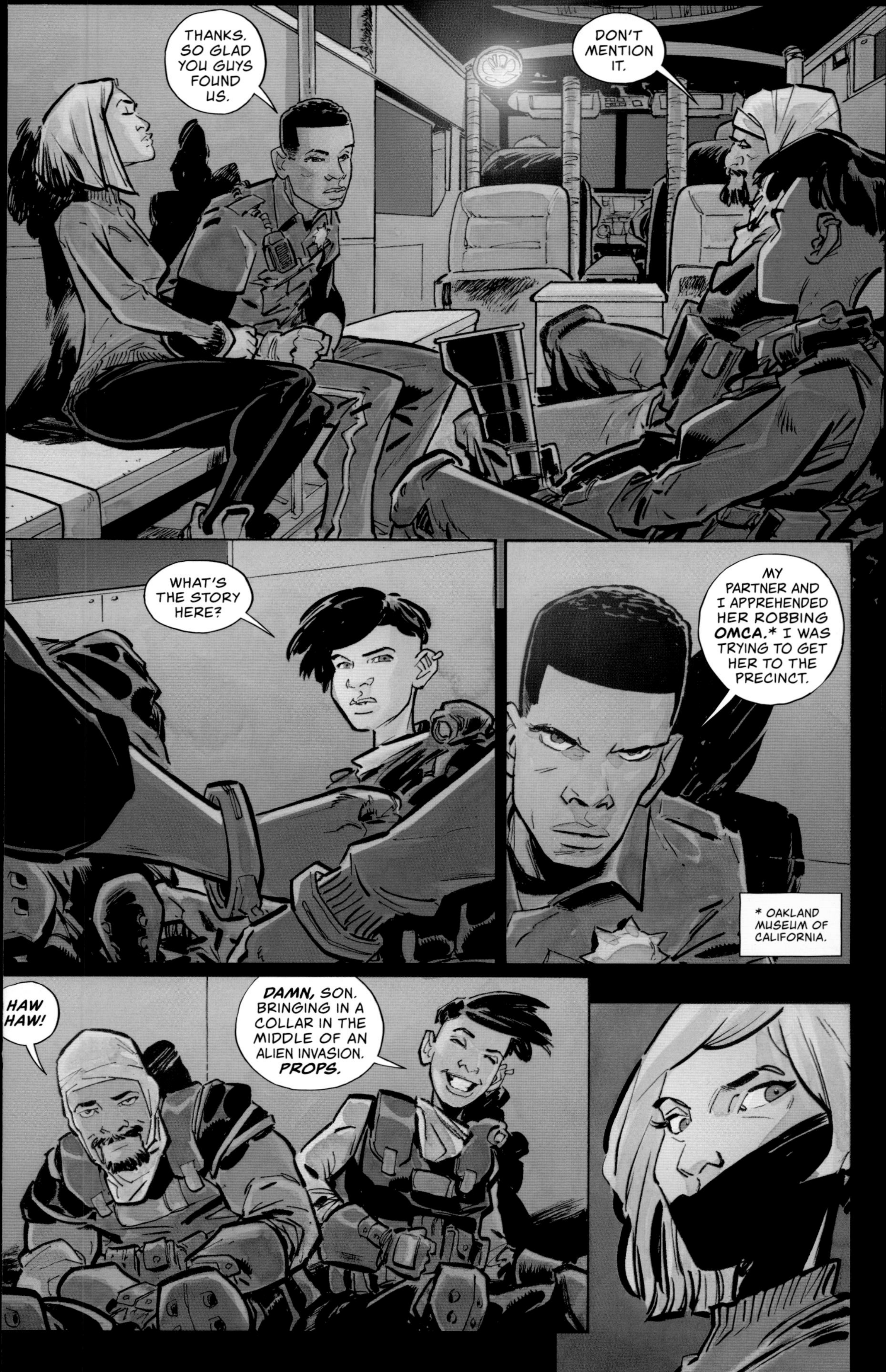
THANKS. SO GLAD YOU GUYS FOUND US.
DON'T MENTION IT.
WHAT'S THE STORY HERE?
MY PARTNER AND I APPREHENDED HER ROBBING OMCA.* I WAS TRYING TO GET HER TO THE PRECINCT.
* OAKLAND MUSEUM OF CALIFORNIA.
HAW HAW!
DAMN, SON. BRINGING IN A COLLAR IN THE MIDDLE OF AN ALIEN INVASION. PROPS.

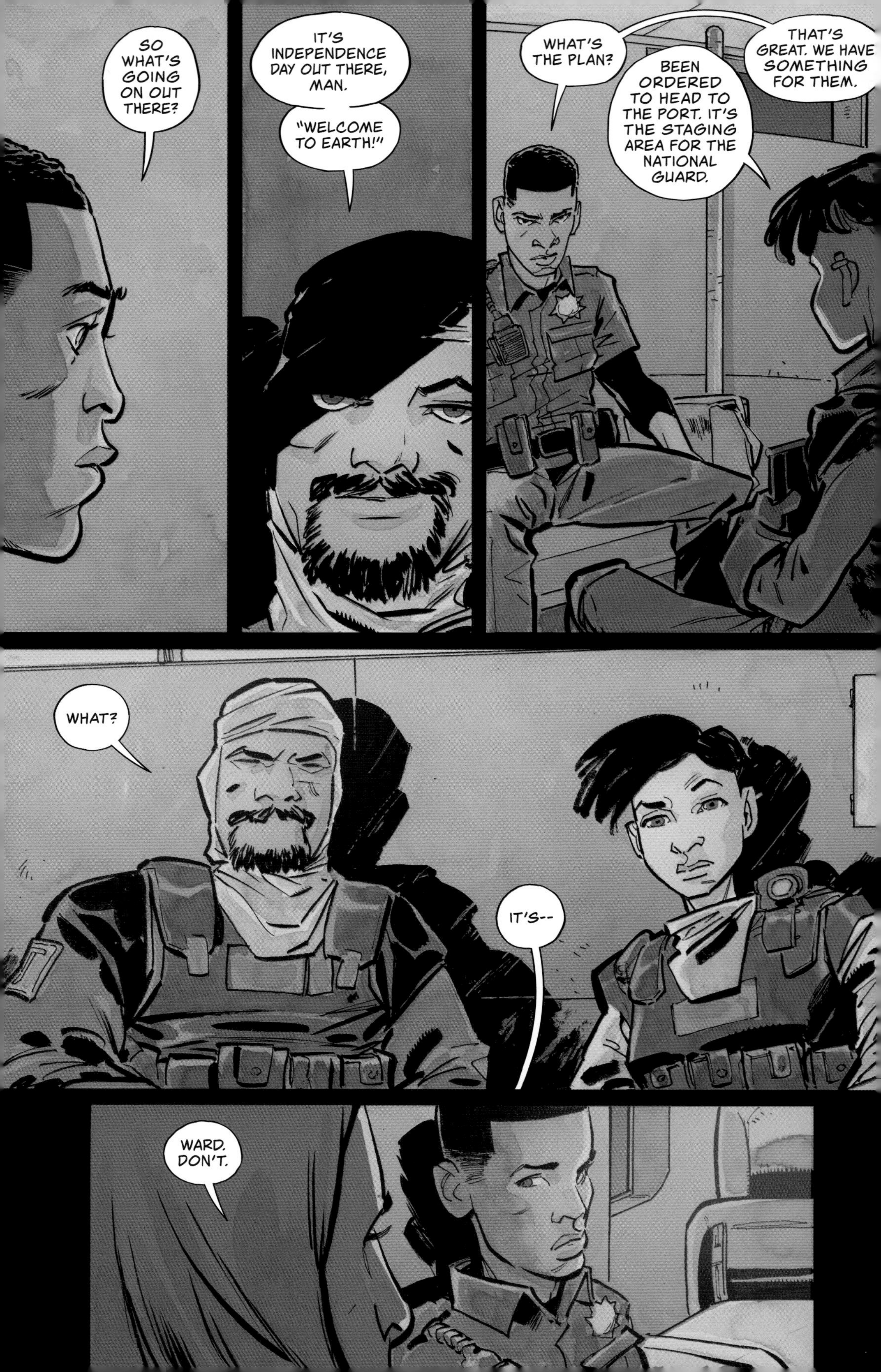
SO WHAT'S GOING ON OUT THERE?
IT'S INDEPENDENCE DAY OUT THERE, MAN.
"WELCOME TO EARTH!"
WHAT'S THE PLAN?
BEEN ORDERED TO HEAD TO THE PORT. IT'S THE STAGING AREA FOR THE NATIONAL GUARD.
THAT'S GREAT. WE HAVE SOMETHING FOR THEM.
WHAT?
IT'S--
WARD. DON'T.

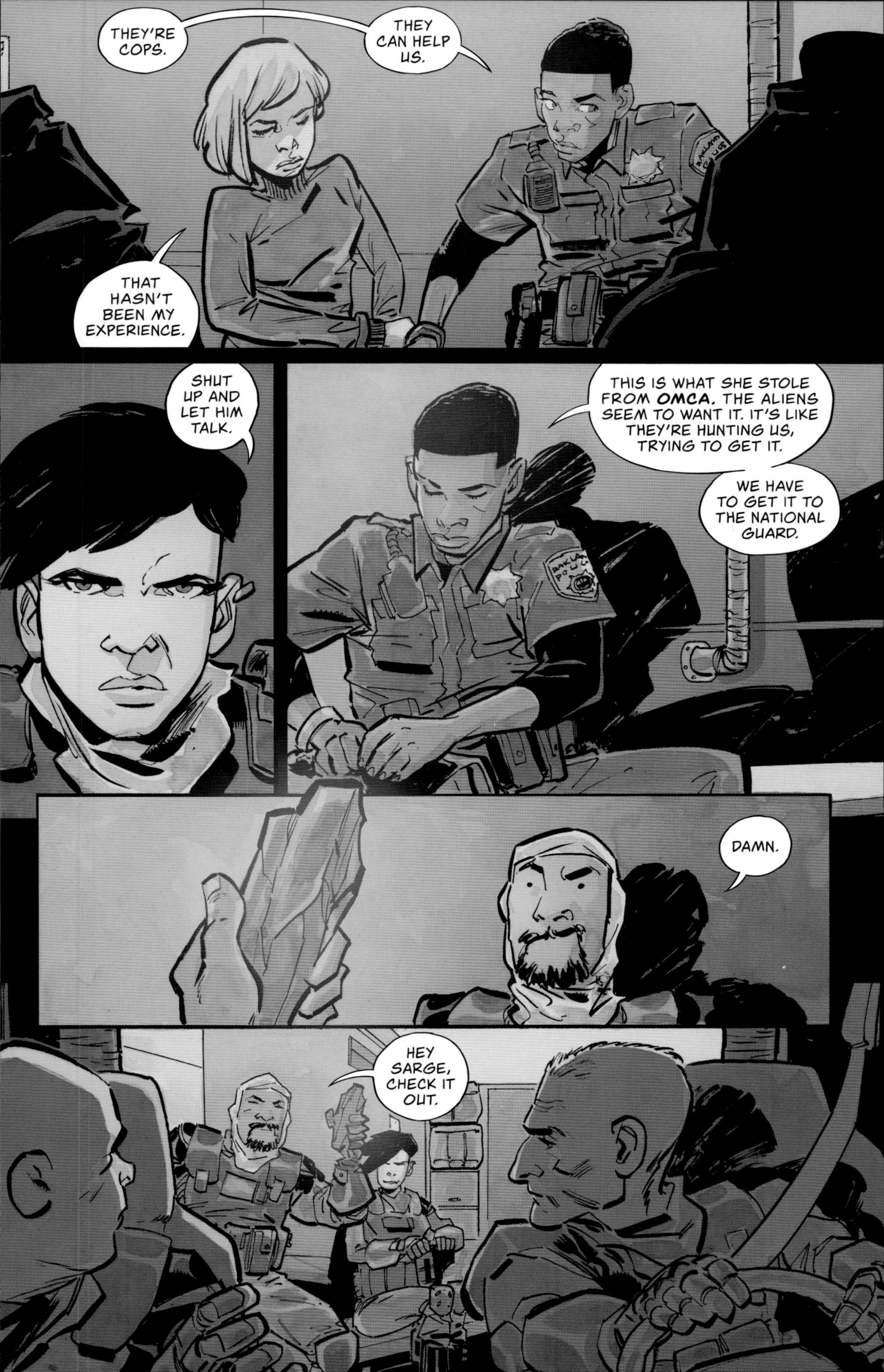
THEY'RE COPS.
THEY CAN HELP US.
THAT HASN'T BEEN MY EXPERIENCE.
SHUT UP AND LET HIM TALK.
THIS IS WHAT SHE STOLE FROM OMCA. THE ALIENS SEEM TO WANT IT. IT'S LIKE THEY'RE HUNTING US, TRYING TO GET IT.
WE HAVE TO GET IT TO THE NATIONAL GUARD.
DAMN.
HEY SARGE, CHECK IT OUT.

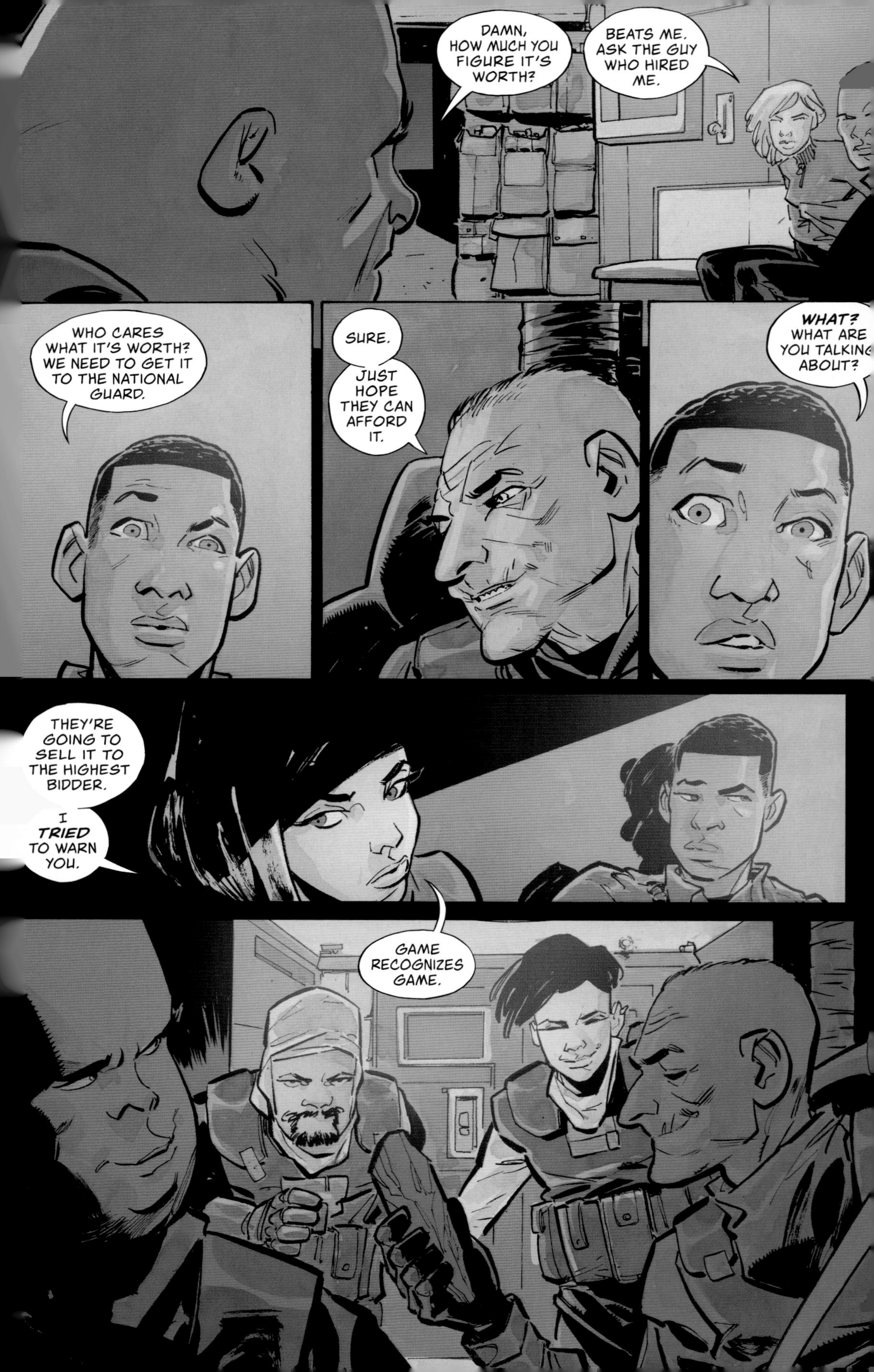
DAMN, HOW MUCH YOU FIGURE IT'S WORTH?
BEATS ME. ASK THE GUY WHO HIRED ME.
WHO CARES WHAT IT'S WORTH? WE NEED TO GET IT TO THE NATIONAL GUARD.
SURE.
JUST HOPE THEY CAN AFFORD IT.
WHAT? WHAT ARE YOU TALKING ABOUT?
THEY'RE GOING TO SELL IT TO THE HIGHEST BIDDER.
I TRIED TO WARN YOU.
GAME RECOGNIZES GAME.

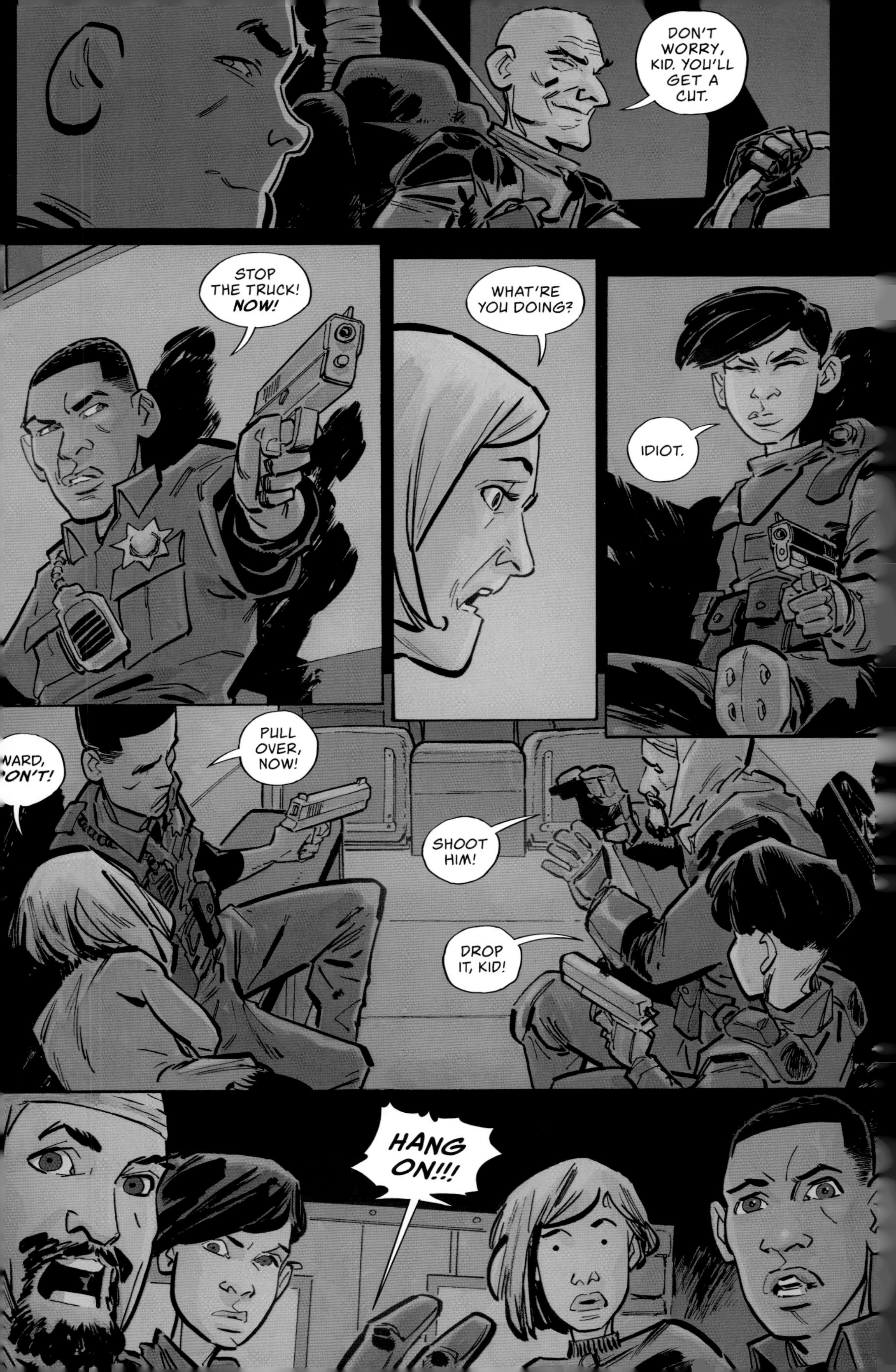
DON'T WORRY, KID. YOU'LL GET A CUT.
STOP THE TRUCK! NOW!
WHAT'RE YOU DOING?
IDIOT.
WARD, DON'T!
PULL OVER, NOW!
SHOOT HIM!
DROP IT, KID!
HANG ON!!!

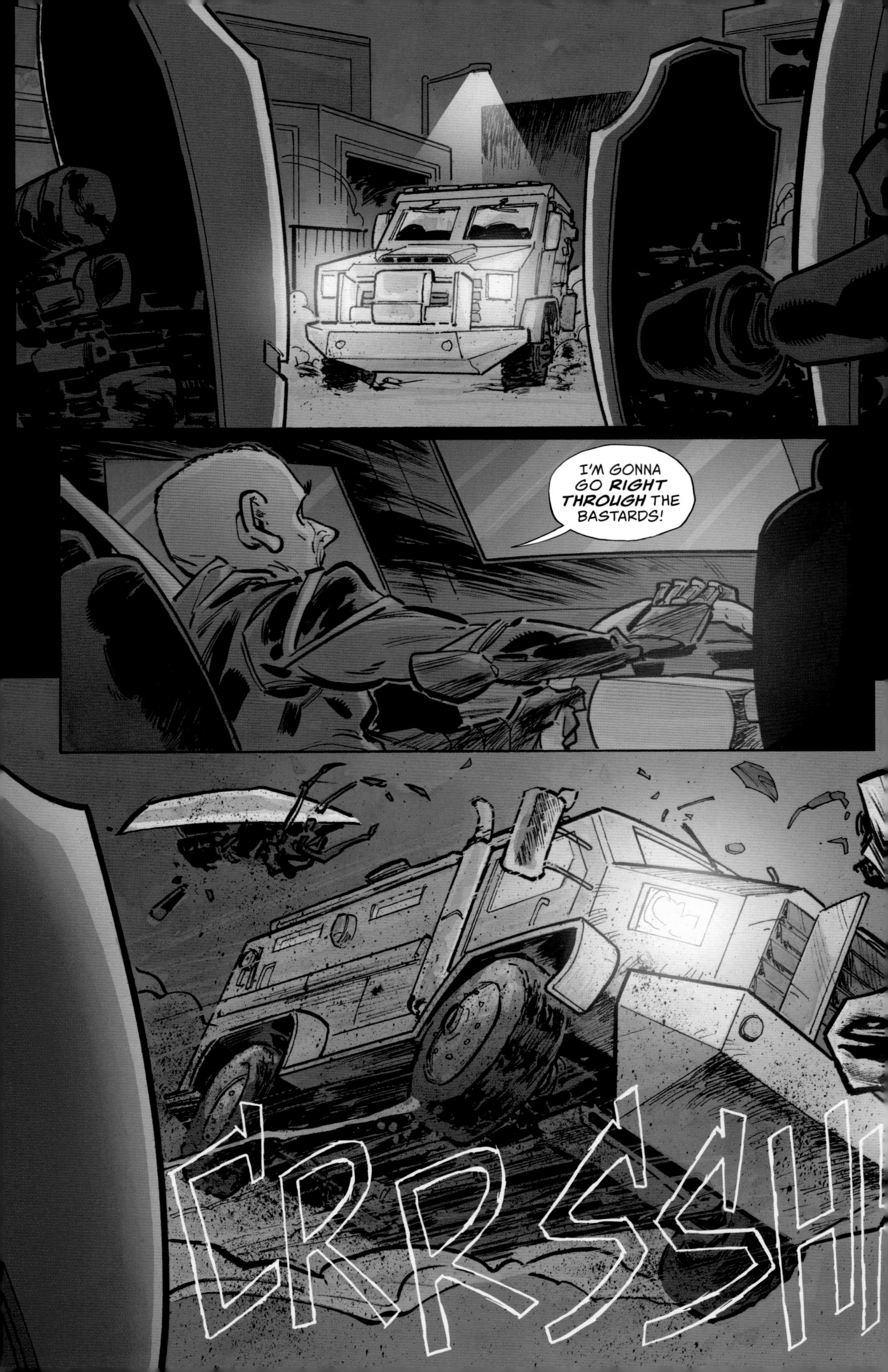
I'M GONNA GO **RIGHT THROUGH** THE BASTARDS!
CRRSSH

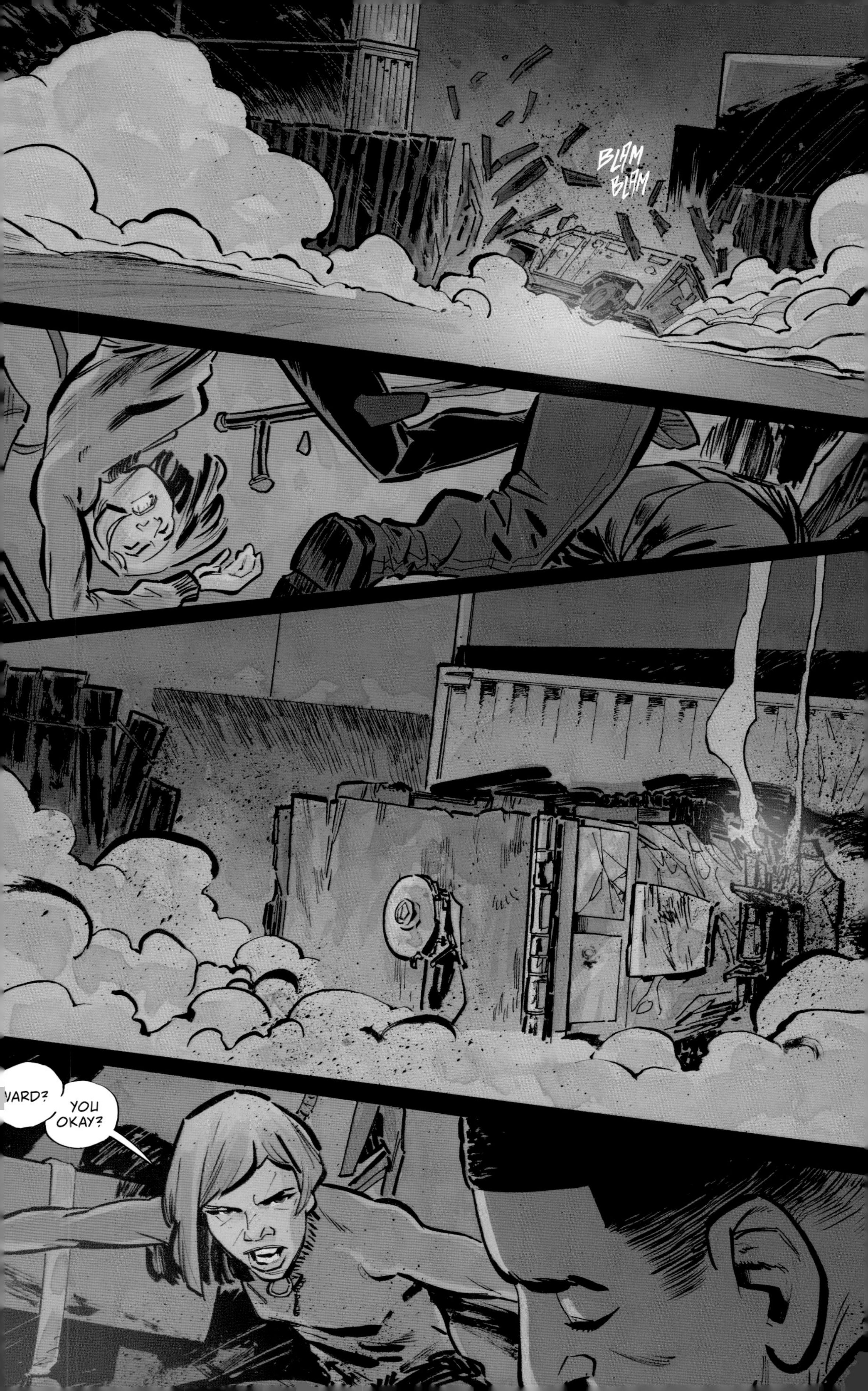
BLAM
BLAM
VARD?
YOU OKAY?

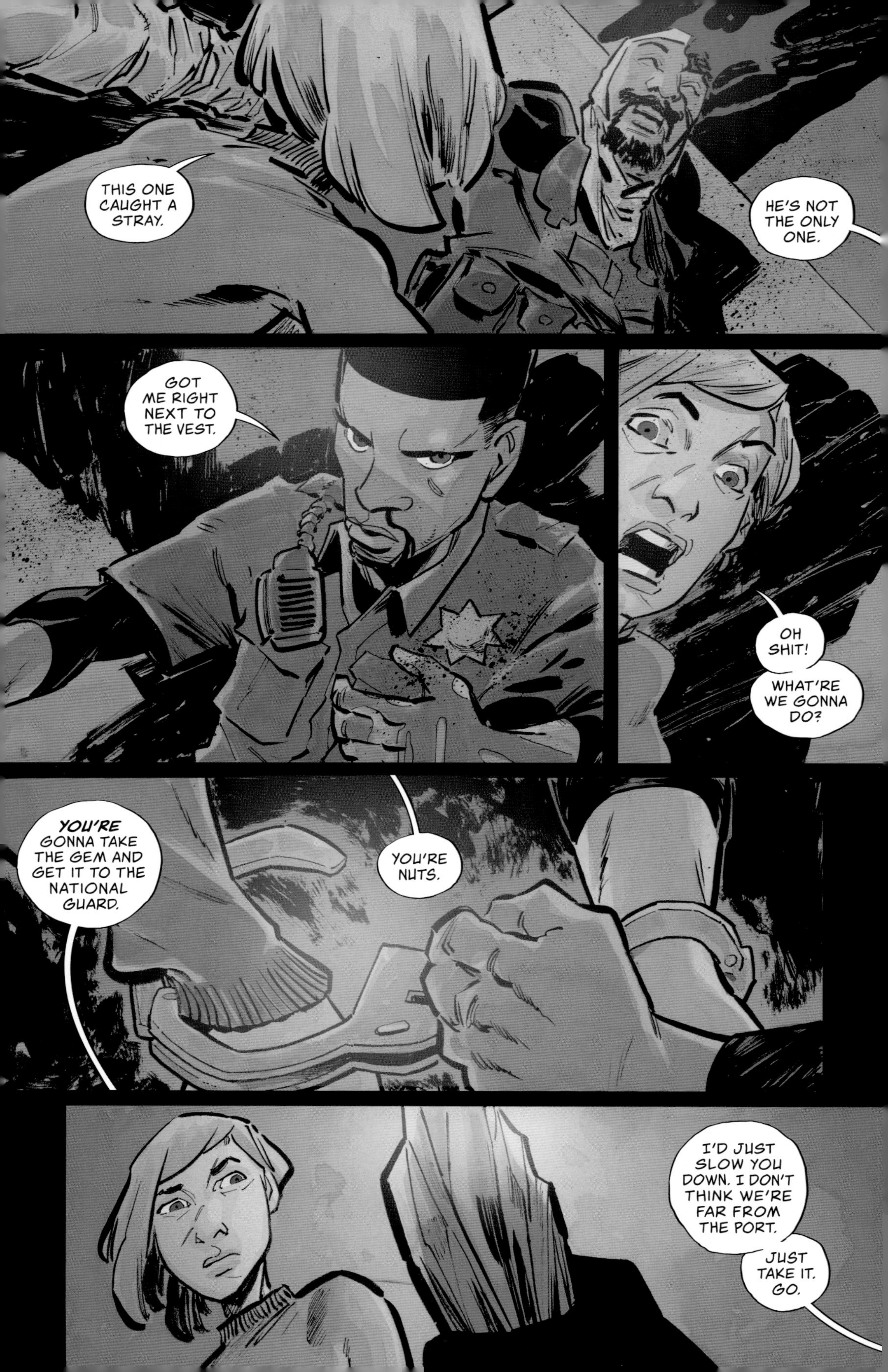
THIS ONE CAUGHT A STRAY.
HE'S NOT THE ONLY ONE.
GOT ME RIGHT NEXT TO THE VEST.
OH SHIT!
WHAT'RE WE GONNA DO?
YOU'RE GONNA TAKE THE GEM AND GET IT TO THE NATIONAL GUARD.
YOU'RE NUTS.
I'D JUST SLOW YOU DOWN. I DON'T THINK WE'RE FAR FROM THE PORT.
JUST TAKE IT. GO.

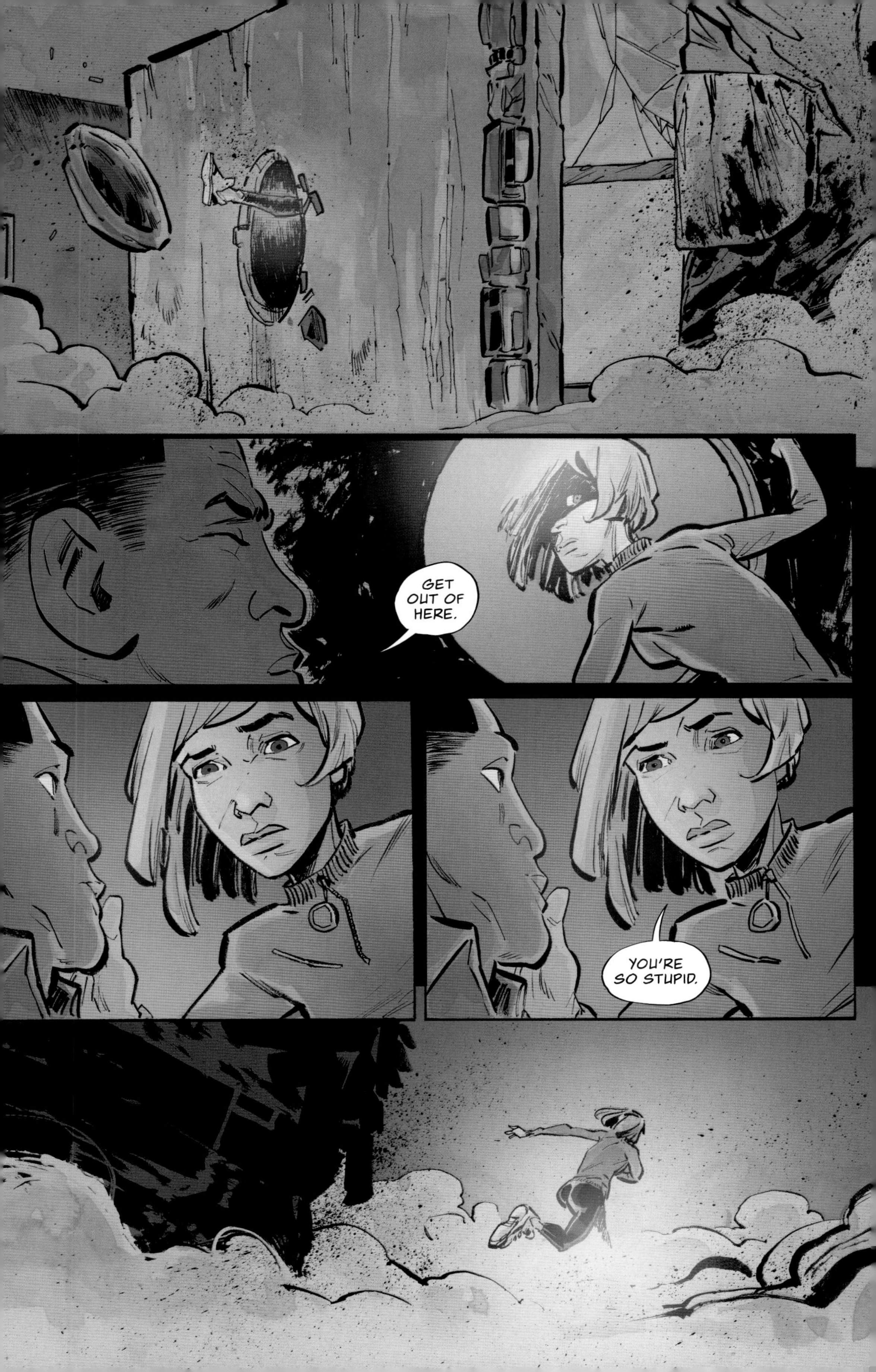
GET OUT OF HERE.
YOU'RE SO STUPID.

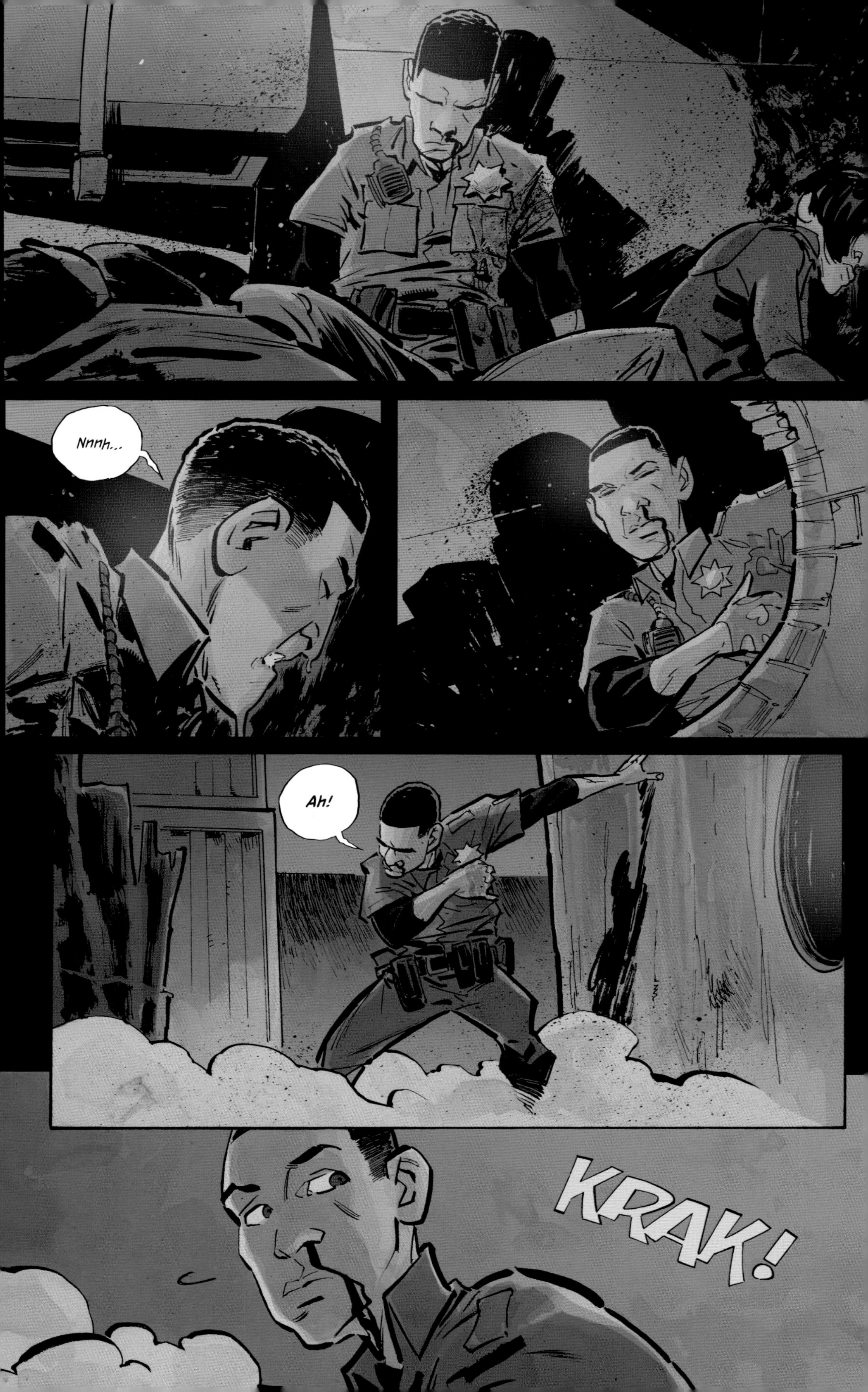
Nnnh...
Ah!
KRAK!

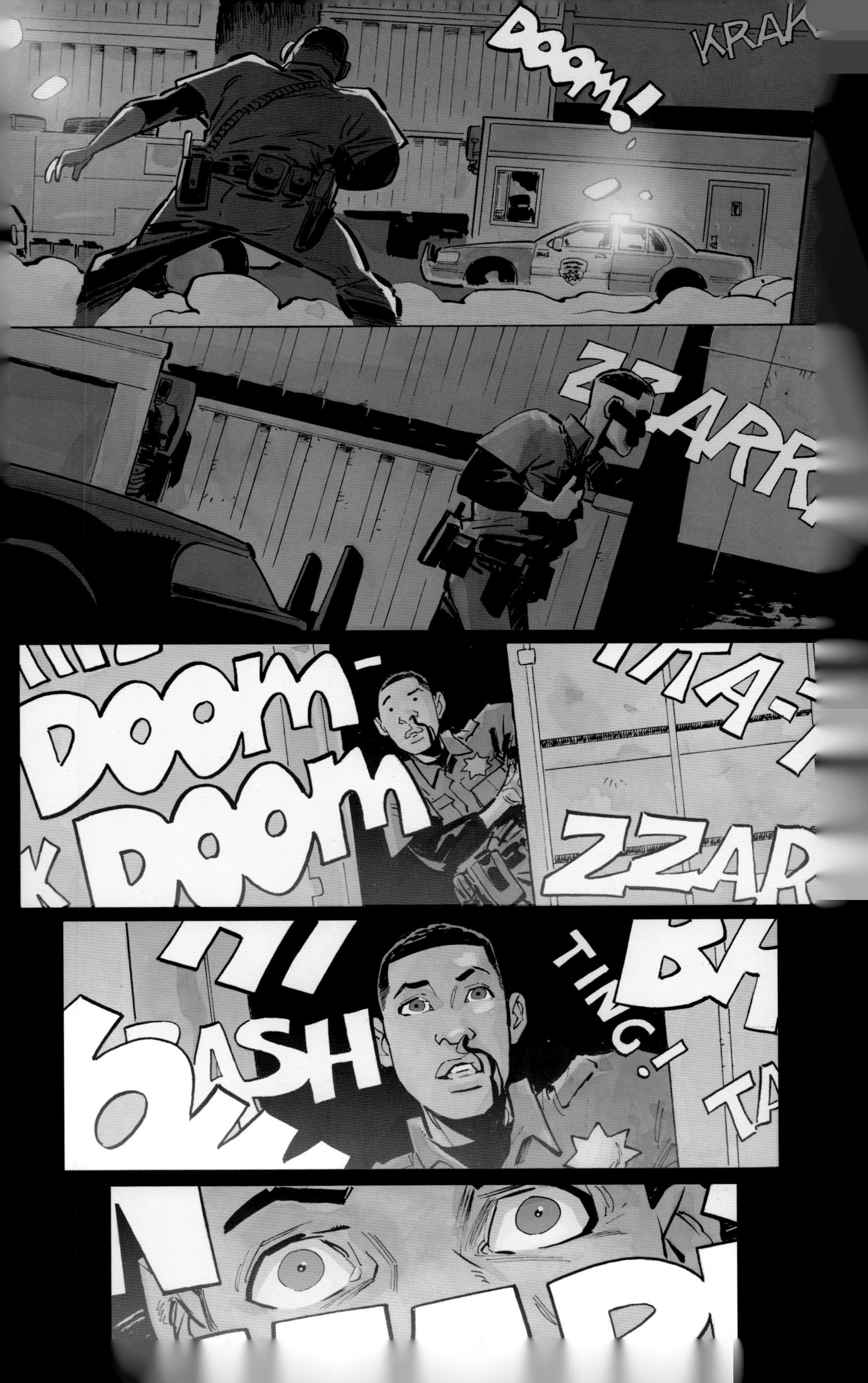
DOOM!
KRAK
DOOM-
DOOM
TING!

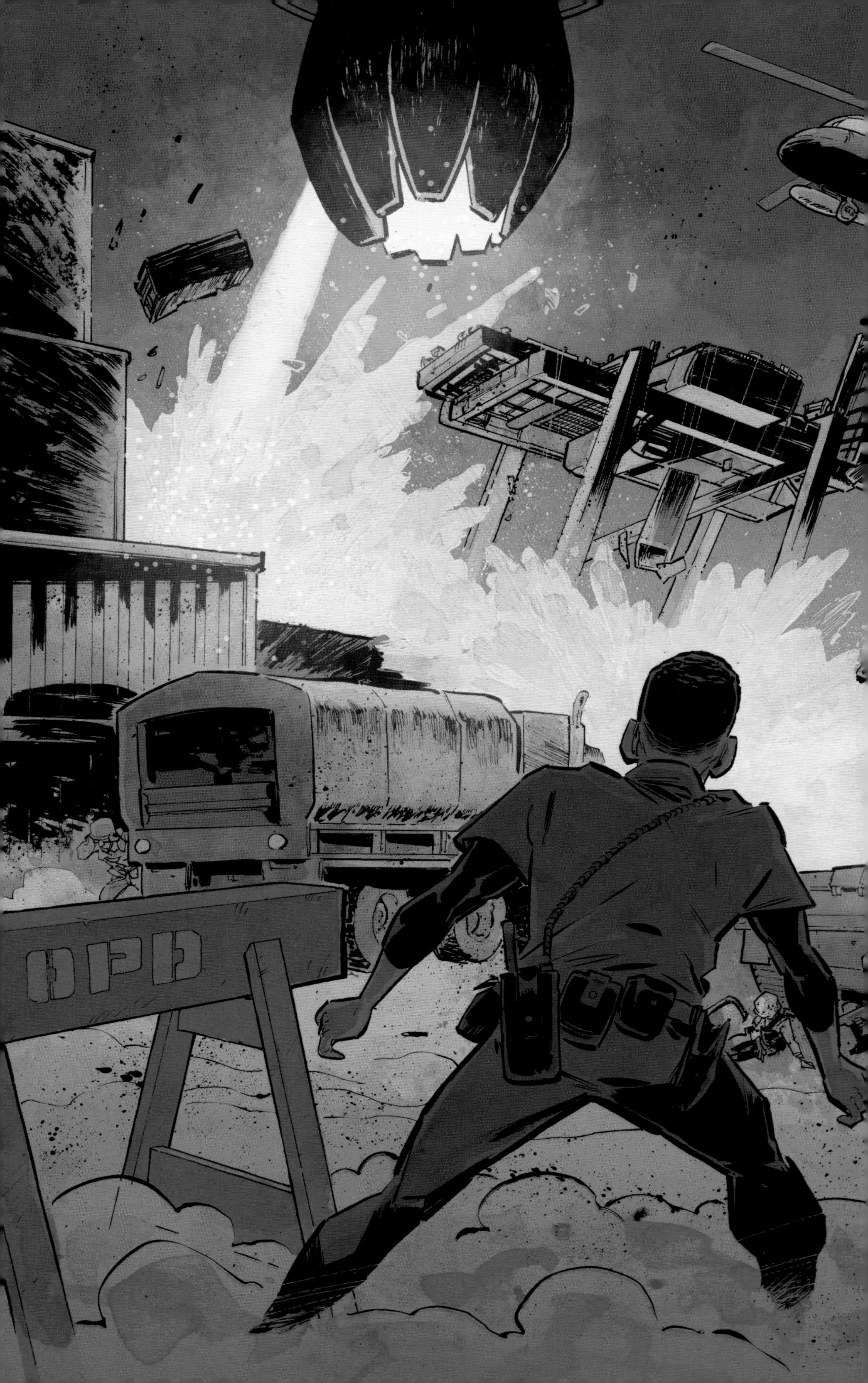
OPD

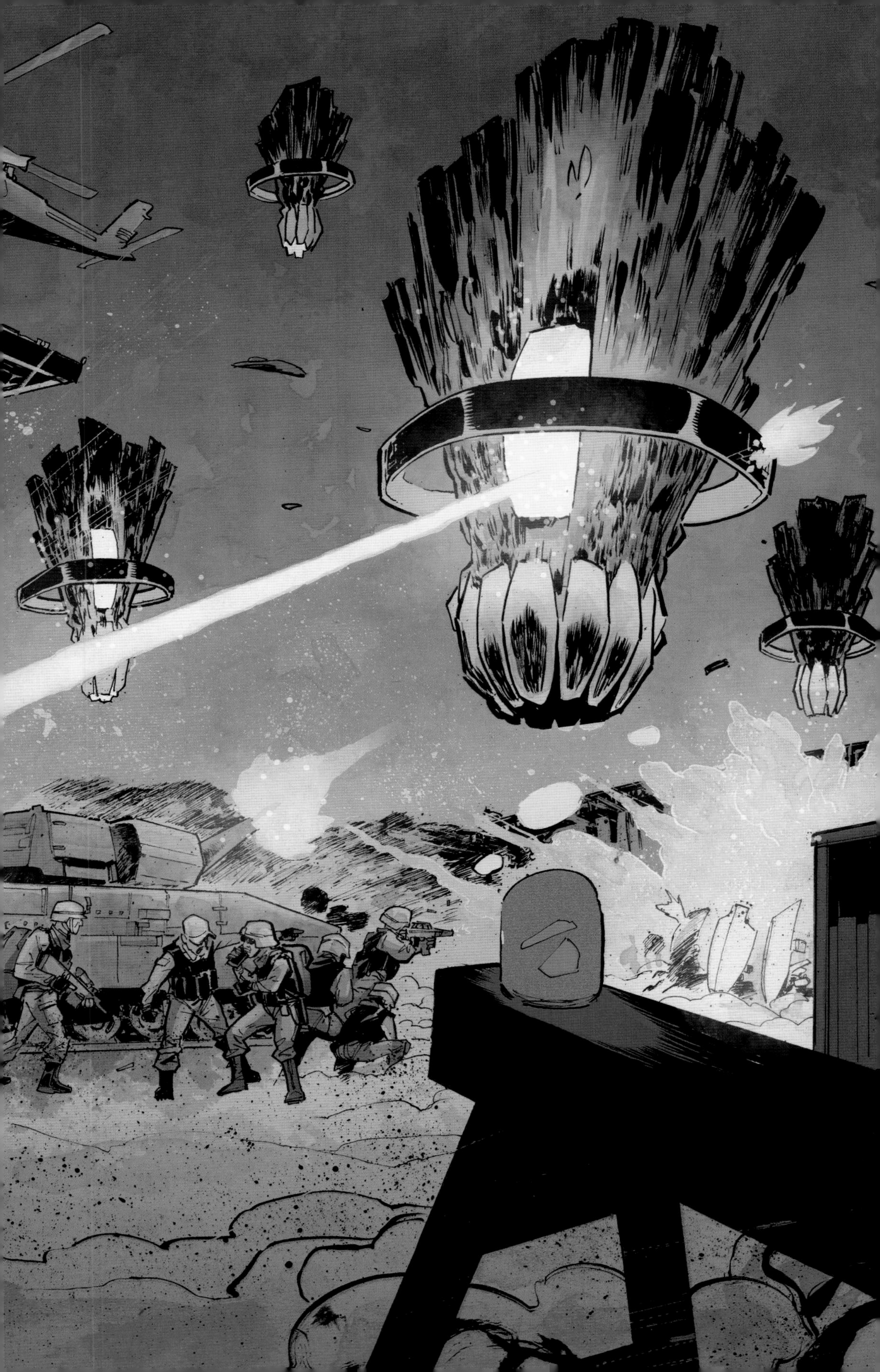

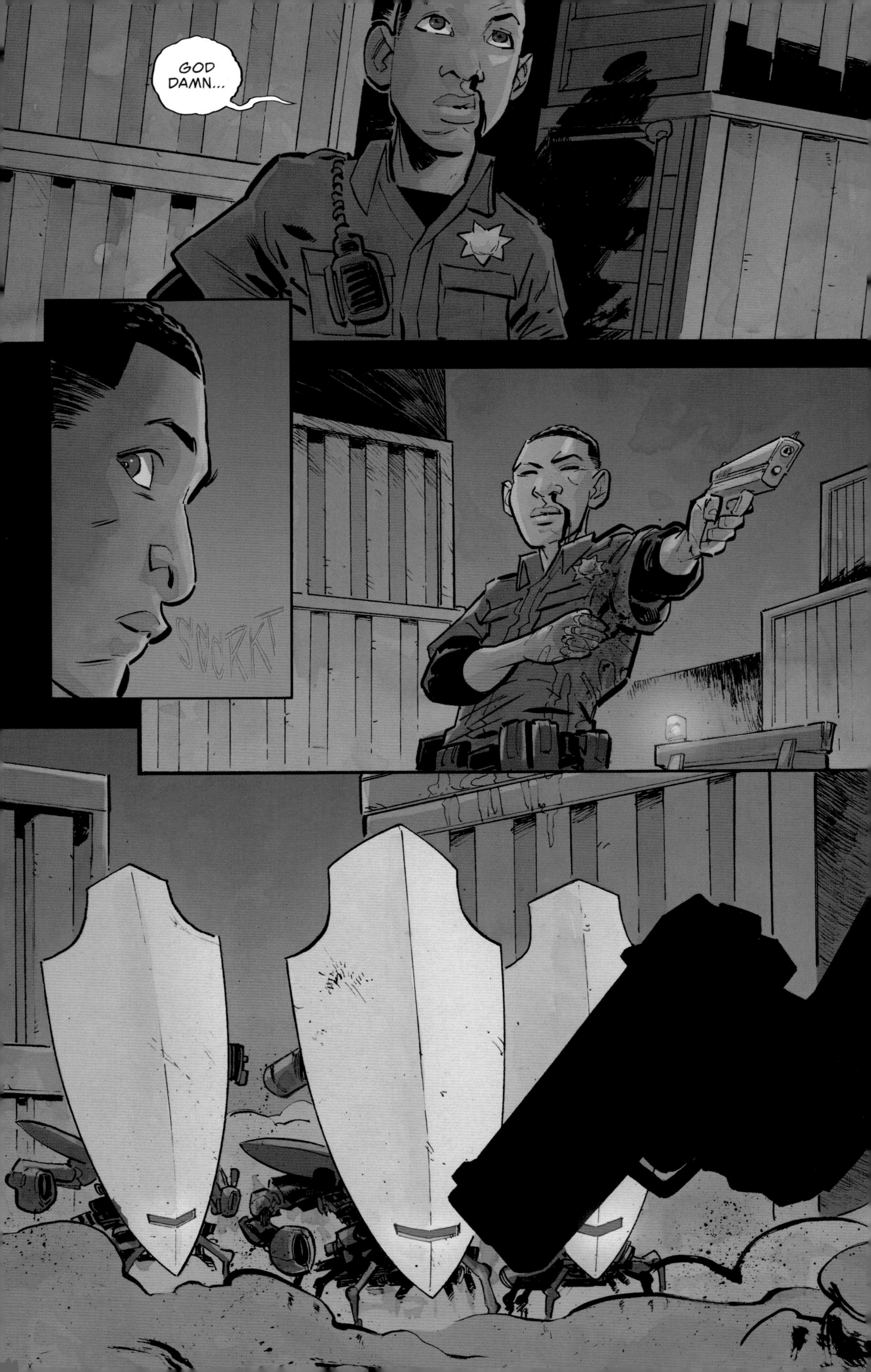
GOD DAMN...
SCCRKT

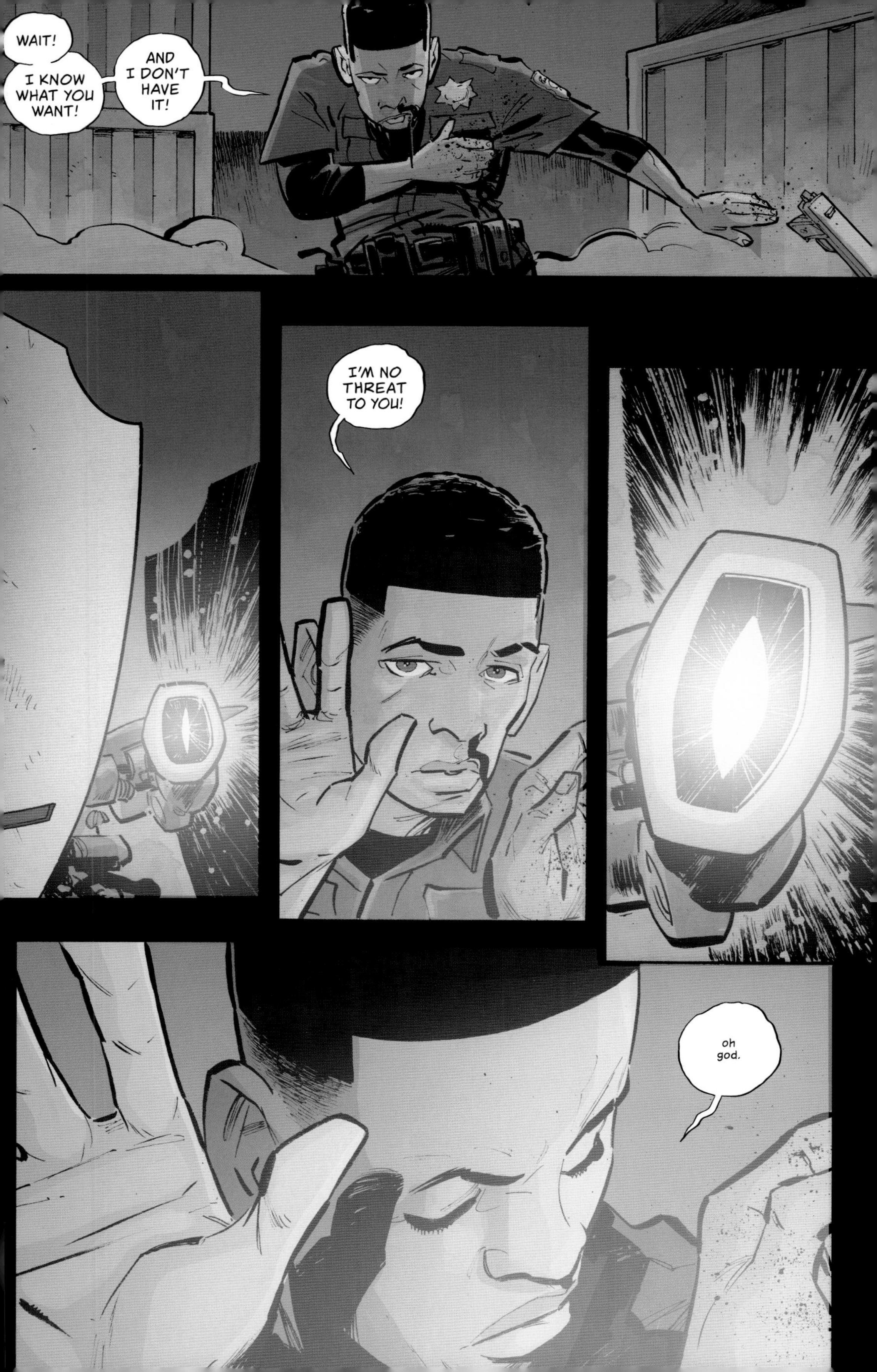
WAIT!
I KNOW WHAT YOU WANT!
AND I DON'T HAVE IT!
I'M NO THREAT TO YOU!
oh god.

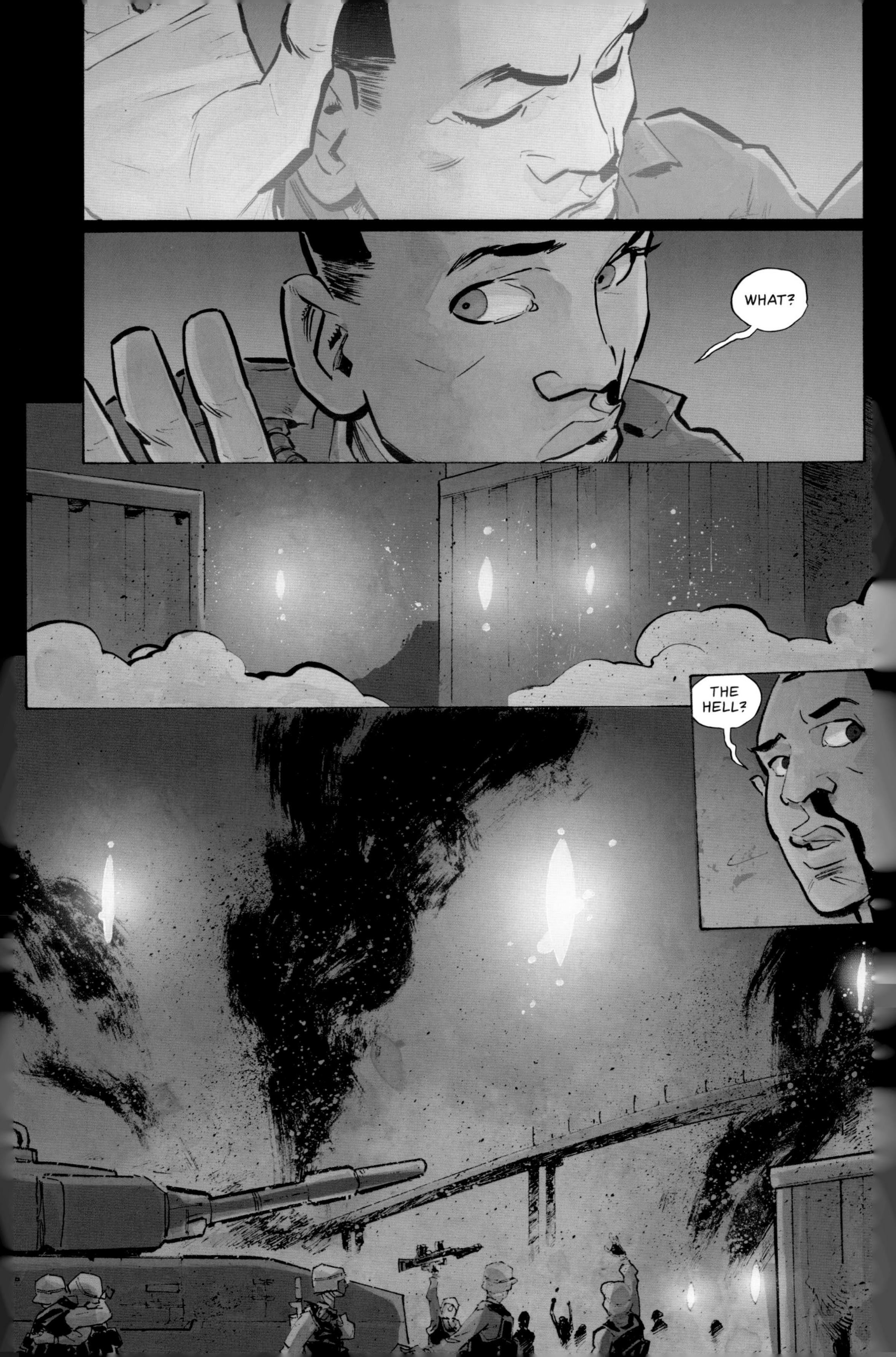
WHAT?
THE HELL?

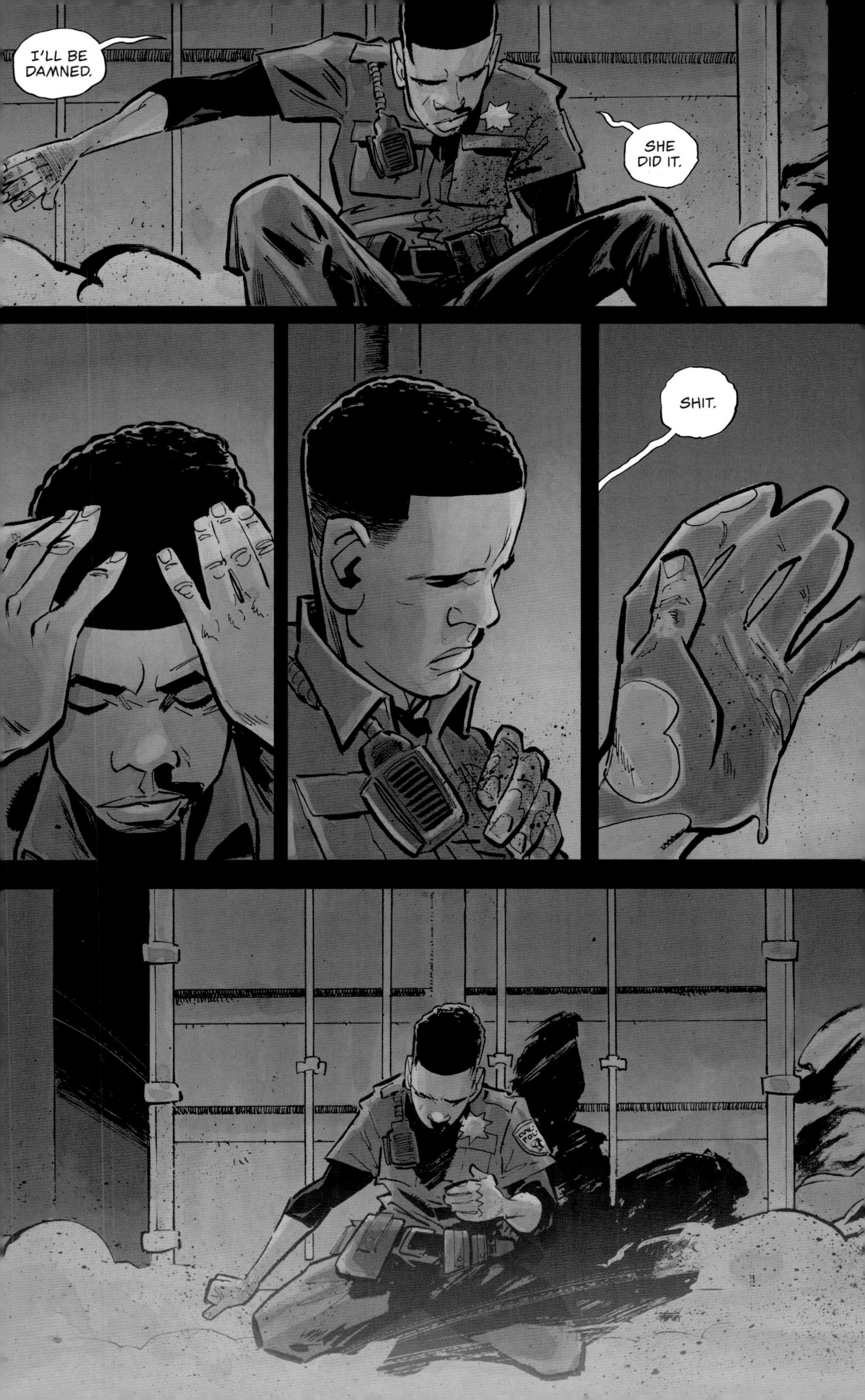
I'LL BE DAMNED.
SHE DID IT.
SHIT.

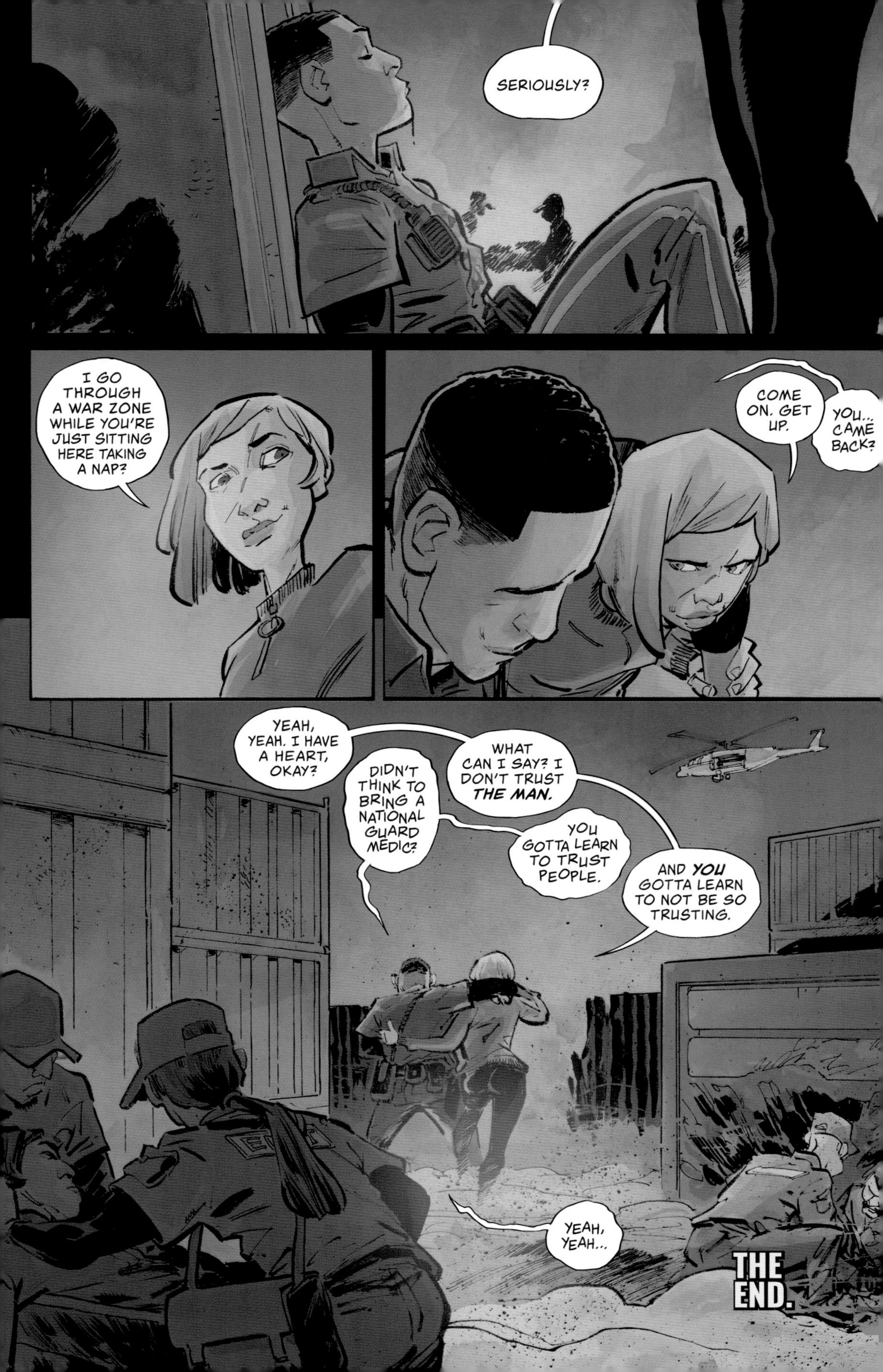
SERIOUSLY?
I GO THROUGH A WAR ZONE WHILE YOU'RE JUST SITTING HERE TAKING A NAP?
COME ON. GET UP.
YOU... CAME BACK?
YEAH, YEAH. I HAVE A HEART, OKAY?
WHAT CAN I SAY? I DON'T TRUST ***THE MAN.***
DIDN'T THINK TO BRING A NATIONAL GUARD MEDIC?
YOU GOTTA LEARN TO TRUST PEOPLE.
AND ***YOU*** GOTTA LEARN TO NOT BE SO TRUSTING.
YEAH, YEAH...
THE END.

BONUS MATERIALS

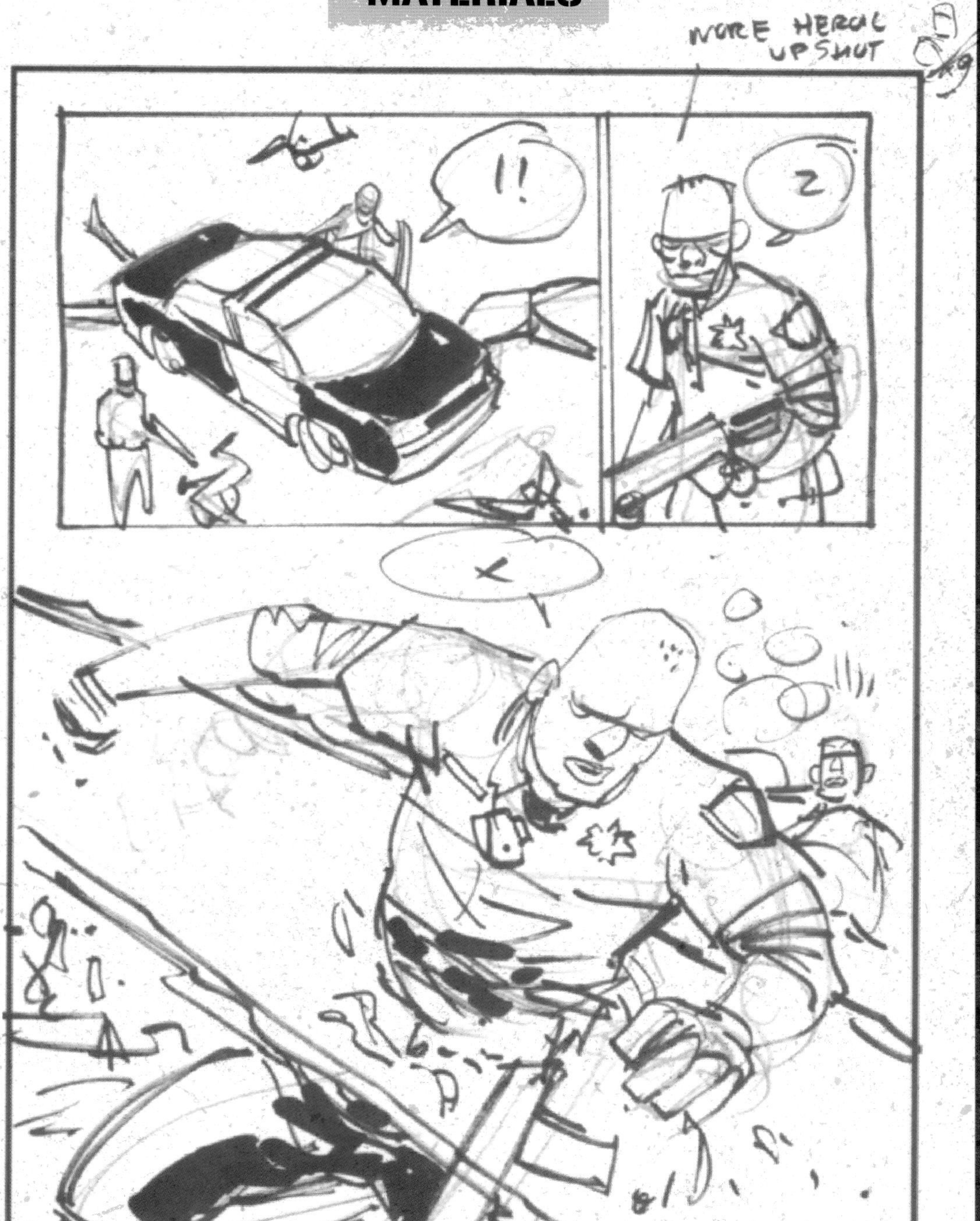
MORE HEROIC UPSHOT
!!

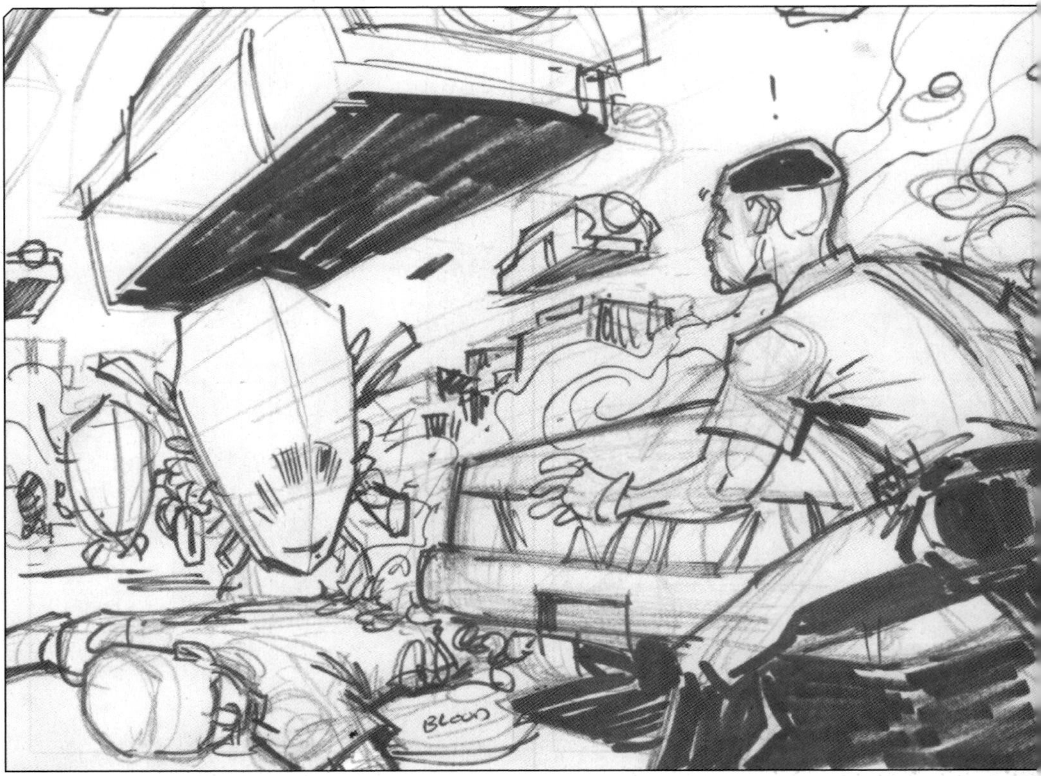
!
BLOOD

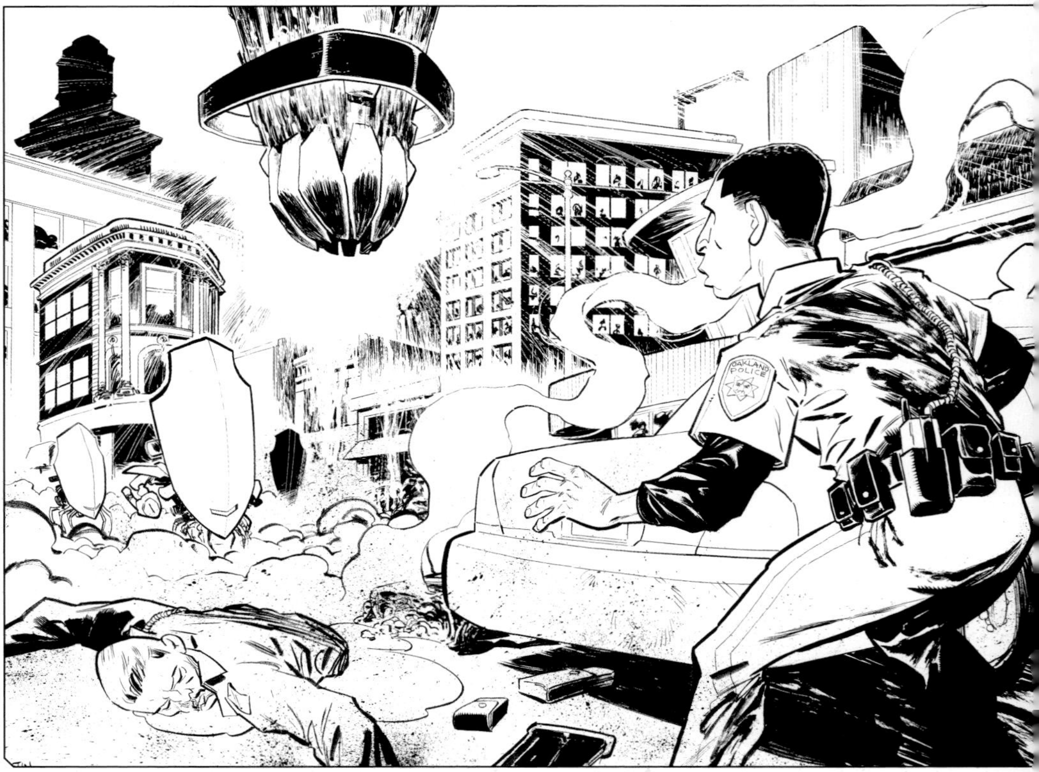
OAKLAND POLICE

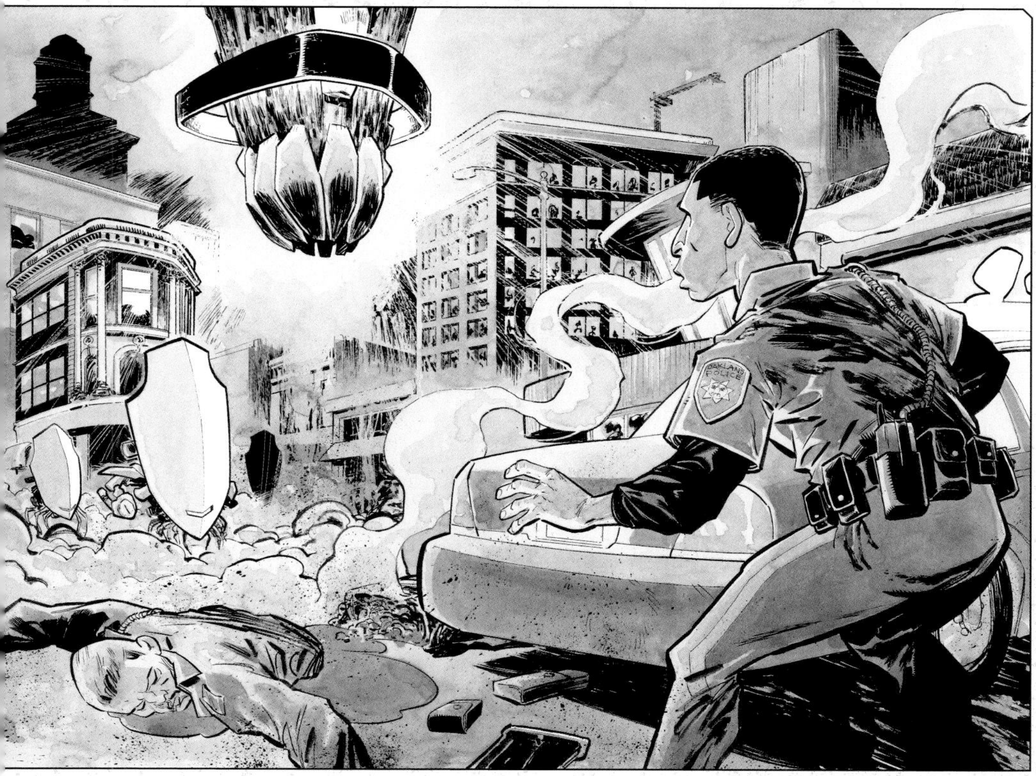

AREA 510

PAGES 12-13 INK WASH

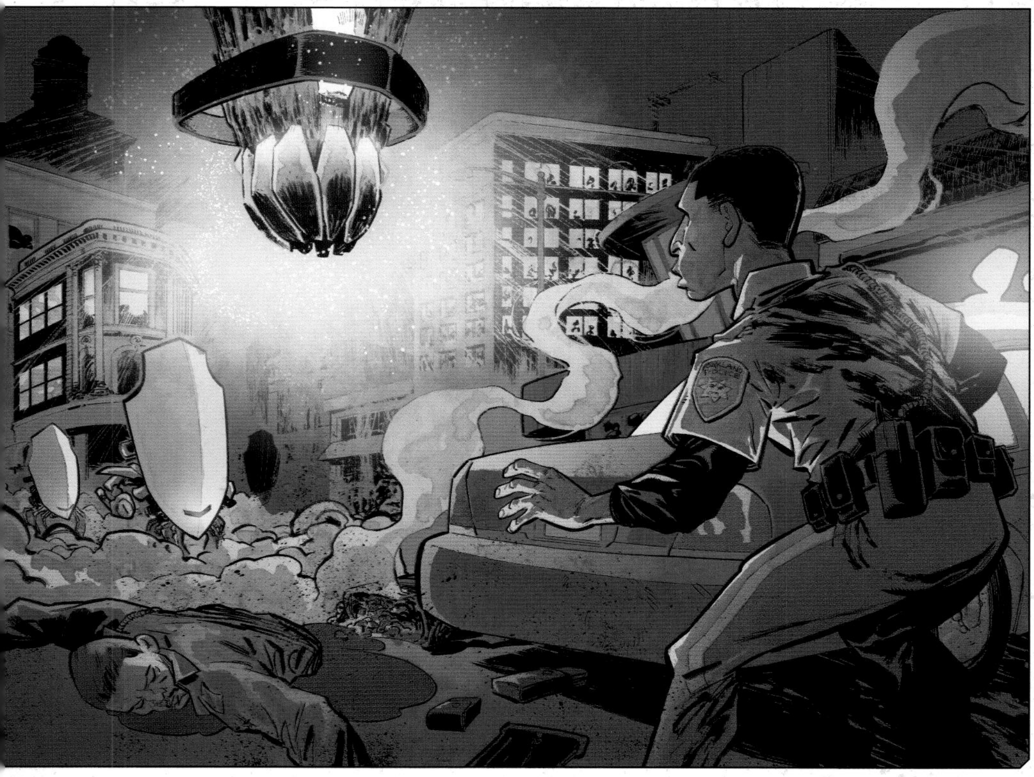

AREA 510

PAGES 12-13 COLORS

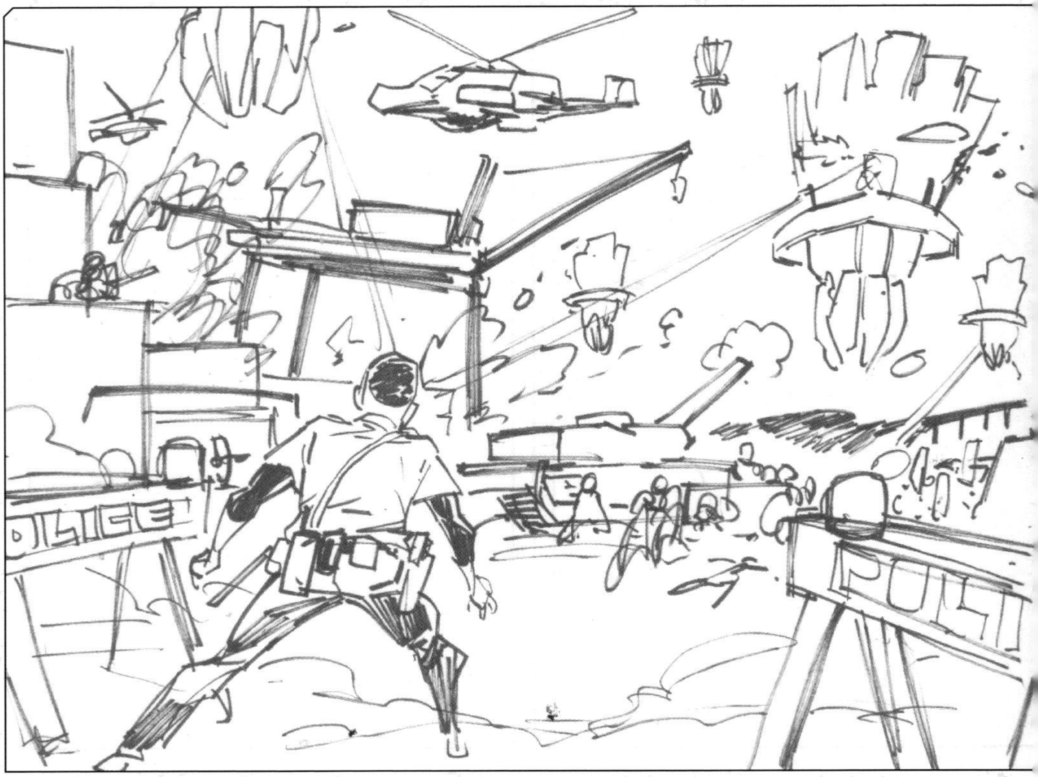

AREA 510 PAGES 52-53 PENCI

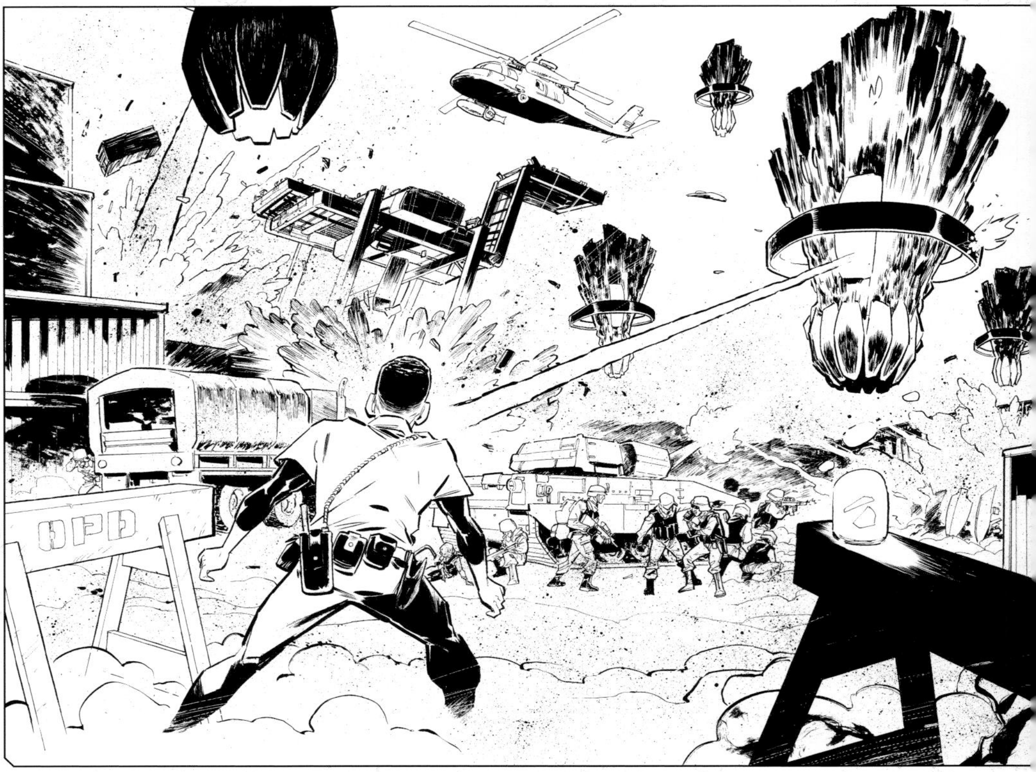
OPD

AREA 510 PAGES 52-53 IN

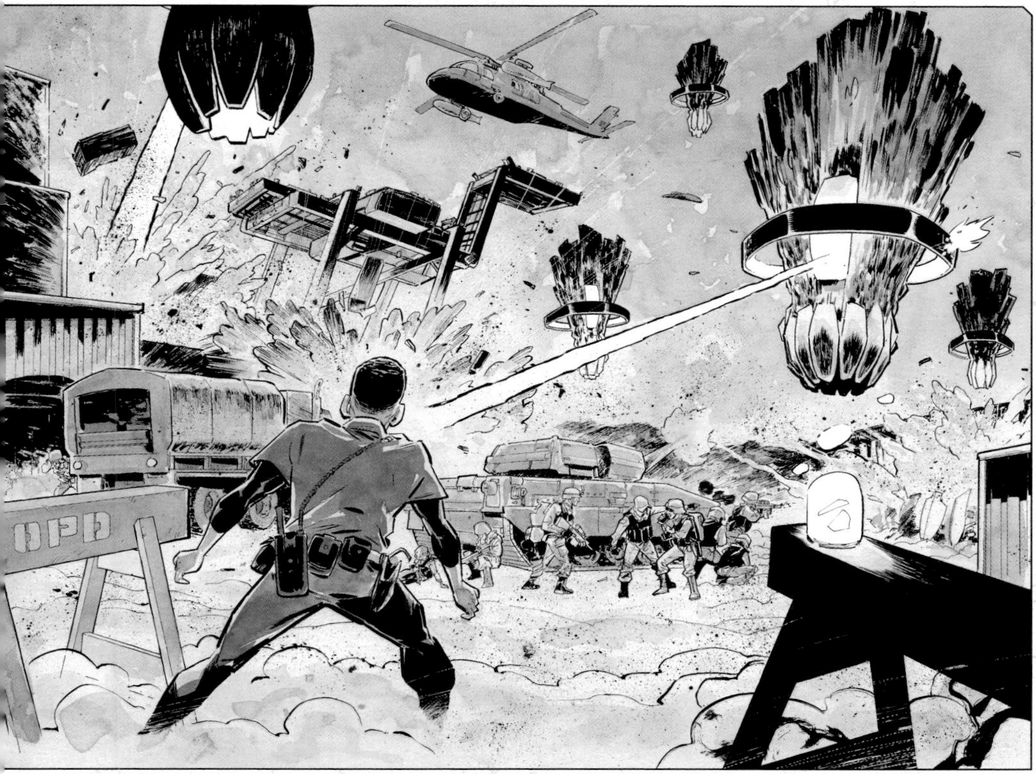
OPD

AREA 510

PAGES 52-53 INK WASH

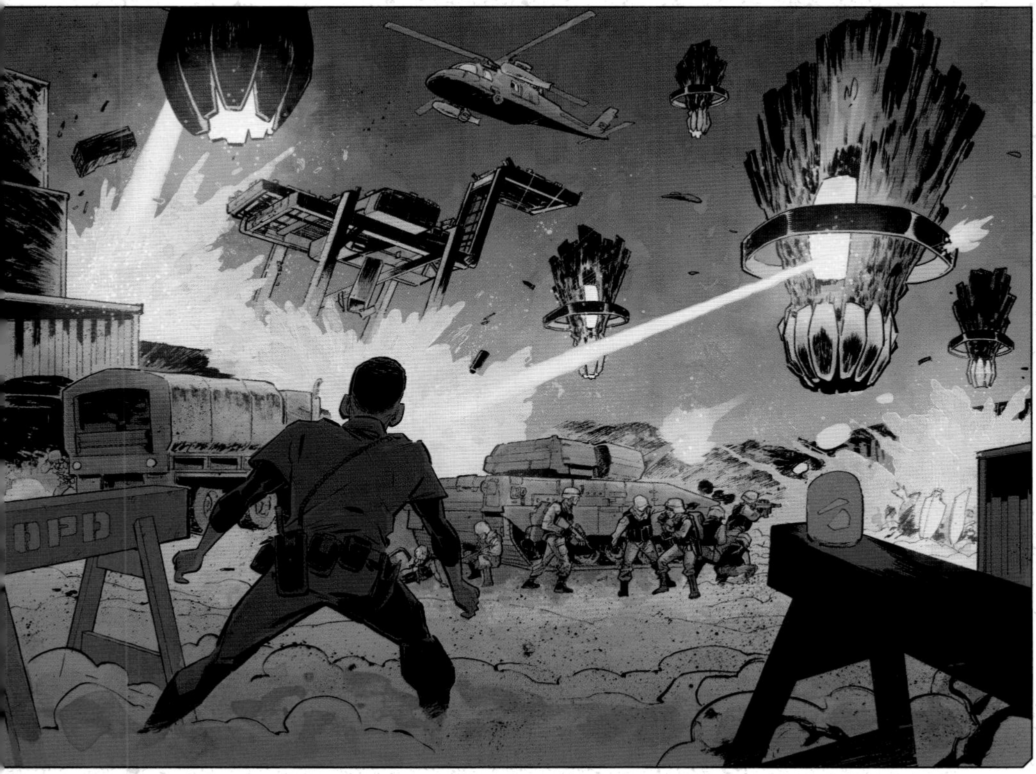
OPD

AREA 510

PAGES 52-53 COLORS

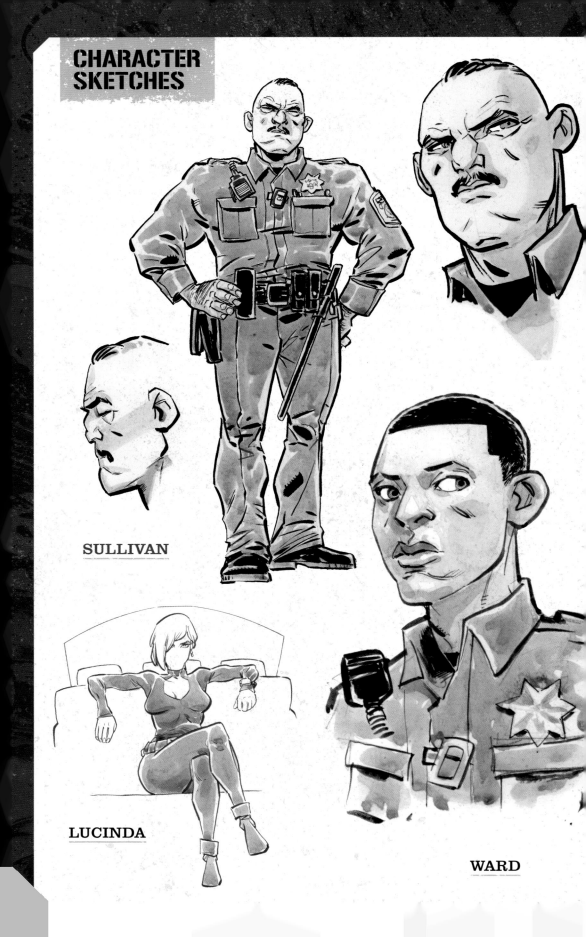

CHARACTER SKETCHES

SULLIVAN

LUCINDA

WARD

WARD

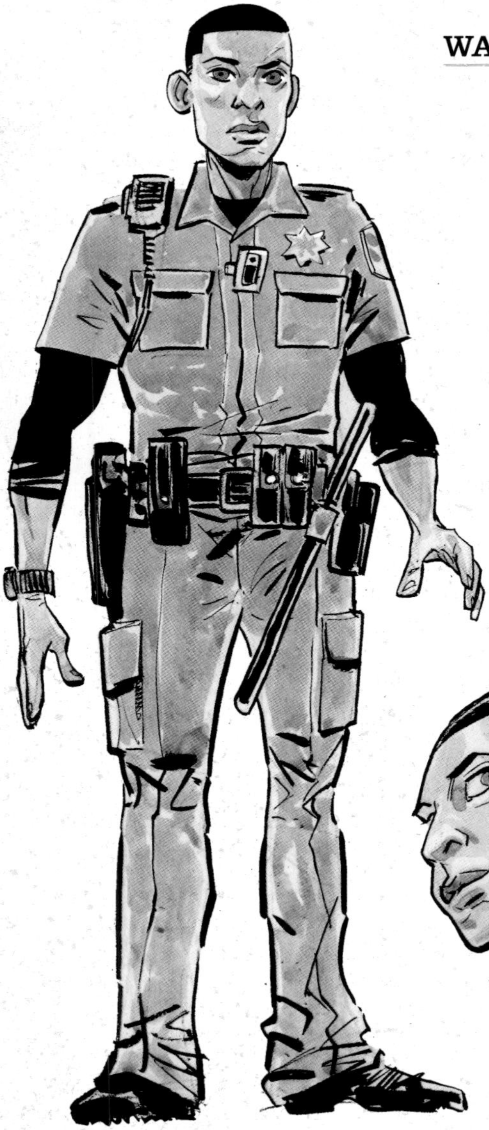

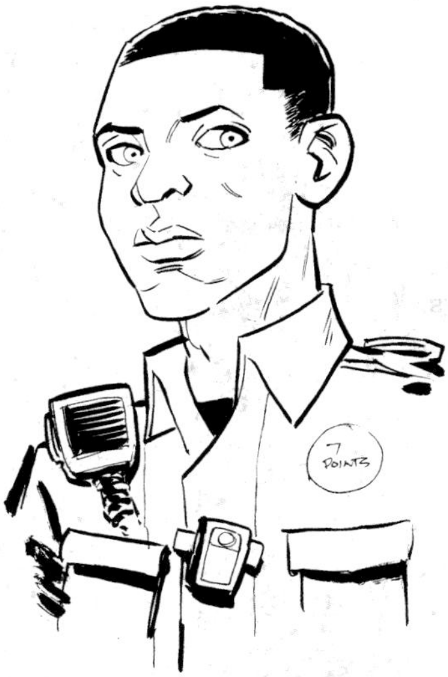
7 POINTS

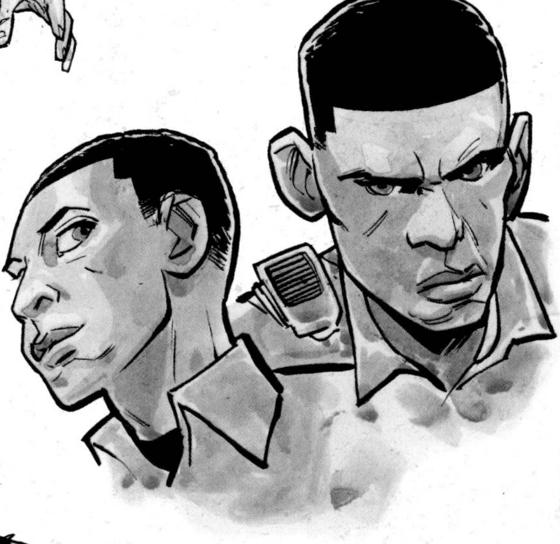

ALIENS

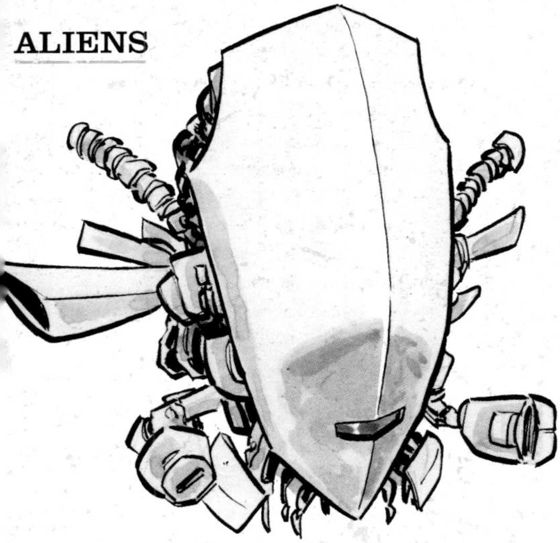

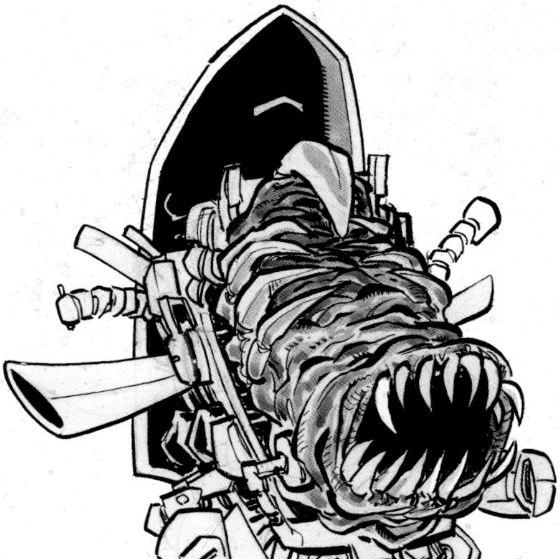

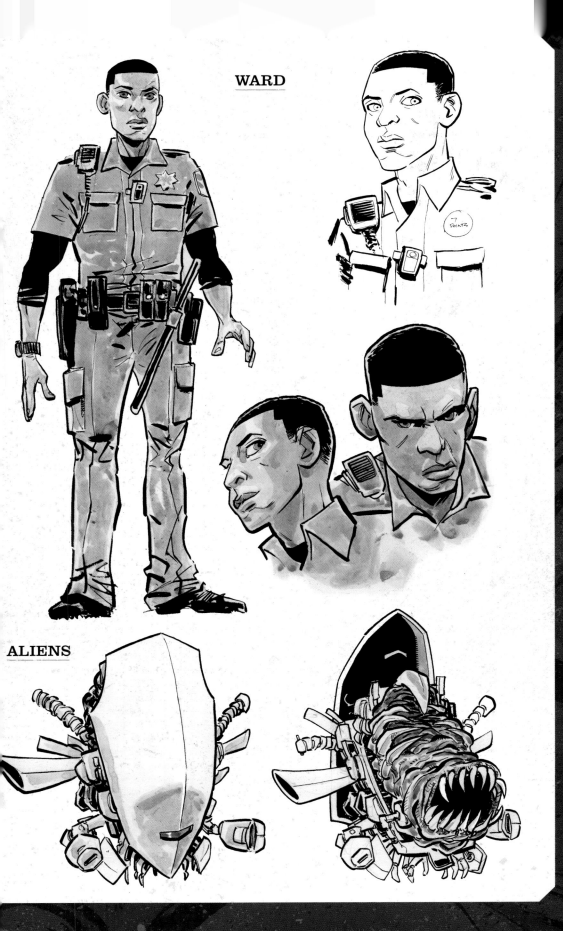

CREATOR BIOS

JAY FAERBER was raised in rural Pennsylvania on a steady diet of comic books and cop shows. After working on various titles for Marvel and DC Comics, Jay wrote and co-created the comic book series *Noble Causes*, *Dynamo 5*, *Near Death*, and *Copperhead*, among others. He has also written for the TV series *Ringer*, *Star-Crossed*, *Zoo*, and *Supergirl*. He lives in Burbank, California, with his wife, son, dog, and cat.

JUSTIN GREENWOOD is an artist best known for his work on comic book series like *Stumptown*, *Compass*, *The Old Guard: Tales Through Time*, and *Crone*. As a freelance artist, he has worked with many companies, including Image Comics, Oni Press, Dark Horse Comics, Ten Speed Press/Penguin Random House, Sideshow Collectibles, Amazon, RadicalMedia, ABC Studios, and the Golden State Warriors. Greenwood was also an executive producer on the ABC television *Stumptown*, based on the Oni Press comic book. When not drawing, you can find him hanging with his wife and kids around the foothills of the Sierra Nevadas.

LEE LOUGHRIDGE is a devilishly handsome man (despite his exceedingly low testosterone) who has been working in the comic industry for well over twenty years. He has worked on hundreds of titles for all the industry's major publishers, his talents on display on every iconic comic book character from Batman to Punisher to Deadly Class and more.

THOMAS MAUER has lent his lettering and design talent to numerous critically acclaimed and award-winning projects since the early 2000s. Among his recent work are Dark Horse Comics' *In the Flood* and *The Dark*; Image Comics' *The Beauty*; and TKO Presents' *Lonesome Days, Savage Nights*, and *The Pull*. He lives with his wife and children near Magdeburg, Germany, enjoys woodworking, and tries to teach himself the five-string banjo.